弗吉尼亚·伍尔夫艺术创作及其作品赏析

朱玉霞　著

中国纺织出版社

内 容 提 要

本书旨在讨论弗吉尼亚·伍尔夫的人生经历、艺术思想和写作技巧及主要作品赏析。第一章着重描述对伍尔夫后来文学发展产生深远影响的生活经历。她出生于一个拥有良好教育背景的家庭，所以从小饱览群书，但维多利亚时代的女孩是没有机会接受正规的学校教育，所以那个时候伍尔夫就注意到女性在生活中的不公正待遇。可见，伍尔夫的女性主义思想的形成不仅是社会环境的结果，而且与她父系家庭教育密切相关。第二章关于国内外学者对伍尔夫的研究，许多学者从不同的角度对她的作品进行了一系列研究，对于进一步研究伍尔夫及其作品有重要的借鉴意义。第三章着重探讨她的女权主义思想，特别是她的“双性同体”理论，她的成就体现在对女性话语权的争取，肯定女性和男性在智力方面的平等性及女性身份的确立。她认为妇女有权享有应有的声望，而不是呆在家里相夫教子。只有男女平等相处，共同努力，才能发展和谐的关系，造福整个人类社会。第四章着重讨论伍尔夫的意识流写作技巧，自由联想，内心独白，象征意象，多重内视角叙述，时空蒙太奇和自由间接引语等六个方面的独特技能，从而以独特的方式揭示人物的内心真实。第五章赏析了伍尔夫的主要作品片段；《雅各布的房间》《达洛维夫人》《到灯塔去》《奥兰多》《海浪》《一间自己的房间》和《墙上的斑点》等部分故事的赏析。

图书在版编目（CIP）数据

弗吉尼亚·伍尔夫艺术创作及其作品赏析／朱玉霞著．-- 北京：中国纺织出版社，2019.11（2025.5重印）

ISBN 978-7-5180-4135-0

Ⅰ.①弗… Ⅱ.①朱… Ⅲ.①伍尔夫（Woolf，Virginia 1882-1941）-人物研究 ②伍尔夫（Woolf，Virginia 1882-1941）-文学研究 Ⅳ.①K835.615.6 ②I561.065

中国版本图书馆 CIP 数据核字（2017）第 241456 号

责任编辑：韩　阳　　责任校对：楼旭红　　责任印制：储志伟

中国纺织出版社出版发行
地址：北京市朝阳区百子湾东里 A407 号楼　邮政编码：100124
销售电话：010-67004422　传真：010-87155801
http://www.c-textilep.com
中国纺织出版社天猫旗舰店
官方微博 http://weibo.com/2119887771
河北晔盛亚印刷有限公司印刷　　各地新华书店经销
2019年11月第1版　2025年5月第2次印刷
开本：710×1000　1/16　印张：8
字数：150 千字　定价：68.00 元

Preface

Virginia Woolf was a prolific writer of essay, review, short story, letter and diary. From 1905, she began and continued for the rest of her life to contribute essays, mainly on literature, and book reviews to newspapers and magazines like *Times Literary Supplement*, *The New Statesman & Nation*, *The Yale Review*, and *The Atlantic Monthly*. Her main achievements are her stream of consciousness and her feminist ideas-androgyny which had great impact on the later literature history.

In the modern twentieth century, new discoveries and development in science, philosophy and psychology did violently shake the steady and recognizable world of laws and rules, which are based on the highly worshiped principles of positivism, rationalism, and realism. Einstein challenged with his theory of relativity, the classical laws of mechanics which then predominated people's general view of the world.

Virginia Woolf is one of the pioneers in literary society. She is commonly understood as a "difficult" writer, because she didn't use a conventional technique familiar to her readers. She was aiming at something new, and she got it. Woolf made a tentative try of this technique in her book *Jacob's Room* (1922), but it is somehow restricted and tentative. But she soon made a success with *Mrs. Dalloway*, which employs a full and free use of stream of consciousness. It's called first success because this was the first time that Woolf had used this writing as her main method and this novel was well appreciated. Later, *To the Lighthouse* (1927) represented a mature express of her innovative writing, where she wrote more boldly and her characters were improved, speaking her peak success with this technique. *The Waves* (1931) went still further with its poetic rhythm and highly symbolic frame, showing a highly abstract consciousness and extreme introspection.

Woolf breaks with the restriction of the traditional feminism. She refers that women have the power to enjoy their due prestige instead of staying at home to serve their husband and children. If a woman wants to write, she must kill the "Angel in the House" so that she can have her own room to materialize her thoughts. What Woolf is more progressive than other feminists lies in her androgynous idea. Only a person has both masculine and the feminine qualities at the same time, can he or she gets success. Androgynous idea was firstly introduced into literature by Woolf in her *A Room of One's Own*. But her most prominent androgynous novel is *Orlando*. The hero Orlando changes his gender from male to female. But after changing his gender he meets with a lot of unequal treatment in life. Actually, this is an epitome of all women in that time. At last Orlando realizes the balance of her masculinity and femininity and gets freedom and love.

Orlando in fact is a miniature of Woolf to show her androgynous ideas that writers must forget their gender in order to accomplish a literary masterpiece. For the society, the gender opposition can only be overthrown after the balance between male and female is reached. In this way a real harmonious society can be built up. This is also the way Virginia Woolf points out for women's liberty.

Woolf's conception was much ahead of her own time and is still of great significance today. Zhu's own research, I should say, is also very helpful both as an academic work in Woolf studies and as a women's voice among Chinese women in their effort towards women's writing and women's emotion. Zhu has been working steadily in her research and it is sincerely hoped that she will make more and greater contributions in her field.

Jiang Hong

Beijing Normal University

2017.9

Abstract

As one of the most famous and successful female writers, Woolf is well-known in China even in the world. Her contribution to the world literature history is significant. This paper aims to get better understanding of her life and her work.

Firstly, this paper is mainly about her special life experiences. She was born in an educated family, so she read a lot of books although she didn't take school education just because she was a girl. From then on, she noticed women's unfair life, which helped her develop her later feminist ideas. We can find that Woolf's feminism is not only a result of the social environment, such as changes in politics, economics and ideology, but also closely connected with her patriarchal tradition. Both social and family backgrounds stimulate the origination of Woolf's feminism. Secondly, the studies about her home and aboard are discussed. Many scholars had some research about her work in different perspectives, mainly on her feminist ideas and her unique writing techniques. Thirdly, the book focused on her feminist ideas, especially her "androgyny". She believed that women have the power to enjoy their due prestige instead of staying at home to serve their husband and children. If a woman wants to write, she must kill the "Angel in the House" so that she can have her own room to materialize her thoughts. Fourthly, the book also concentrated on her unique skills of stream of consciousness in six aspects such as free association, symbolic imagery, "multiple inner points of view" narration, shuffle of time and space, the free in direct speech. Finally, her major books are discussed, along with the stories appreciation, including *Jacob's Room*, *Mrs. Dalloway*, *To the Lighthouse* and *Orlando*, *The Waves*, *A Room of One's Own*, *The Mark on the Wall.* From these books we can appreciate her ideas and writing skills.

Contents

Chapter One The Life Story of Virginia Woolf

Adeline Virginia Woolf (January 25, 1882 – March 28, 1941), an English author, essayist, publisher, and writer of short stories, was regarded as one of the foremost modernist literary figures of the twentieth century. During the interwar period, she was a significant figure in London literary society and a member of the Bloomsbury Group. [1] Her most famous works include the novels *Mrs Dalloway* (1925), *To the Lighthouse* (1927) and *Orlando* (1928), and the book-length essay *A Room of One's Own* (1929), with its famous dictum, "A woman must have money and a room of her own if she is to write fiction." Virginia Woolf is not only a famous critic, essayist, novelist, and biographer, but also a prominent precursor of modern feminist literary criticism of the twentieth century. She was born at Hyde Park Gate[2] in 1882, the little daughter of the eminent editor and critic, Sir Leslie Stephen, and his wife Julia Jackson Duckworth. She grew up in a cultured and literary atmosphere, receiving her education from the tutor and her father's extensive library, while her brothers were sent to the public schools and then to Cambridge to receive the best education. Virginia Woolf was extremely conscious of the disadvantages of not being well educated. After the death of her mother, Virginia Woolf suffered the first major breakdown in 1904. Afterwards she settled in the Bloomsbury district of London with her brother Thoby and sister Vanessa, and soon she became a central figure of the Bloomsbury Group, where she met Leonard Woolf, who later became her husband in 1912. Her first two novels, *The Voyage Out*, which appeared in 1915, and *Night and Day*, which appeared in 1919, were fairly conventional literary works. But *Jacob's Room*, which appeared in 1922, the highly experimental and impressionistic work launched Virginia Woolf as an innovative writer. "Her modernist approach of using the interior monologue, or 'stream of consciousness', and poetic symbolism, with the emphasis on character as opposed to plot, was developed further in her later novels: *Mrs. Dalloway* (1925), *To the Lighthouse*

(1927), *The Waves* (1931) and the posthumously published *Between the Acts* (1941)." As a female writer in the male-dominated society, she was concerned about woman's experience very much. Her feminist literary volumes were *Orlando*: *A Biography* (1928), *A Room of One's Own* (1929), and *Three Guineas* (1938). The later feminists appraised these feminist texts highly.

1.1 Her Early Life

She was born at Hyde Park Gate in 1882, the little daughter of the eminent editor and critic, Sir Leslie Stephen, and his wife Julia Jackson Duckworth. It was from this huge family that Virginia got nurtured to grow as a prominent writer, but also from this complex connections, she tasted patriarchal oppression at an early age.

Though Leslie was respected and admired by his daughters, his abuse and domination irritated his daughters, who later regarded him as a domestic tyrant. Despite of his brilliance and courage, Leslie demanded emotional protection and shelter from the outside world. Virginia had seen how her mother worn out under her father's endless demands. After her mother's death at the age of 49, this burden naturally fell onto the daughters of the family—other women in the house who were supposed to give sympathy and care to the family member.

However, she might respect his various gifts and achievements objectively. She still felt in an organic sense that his dominating presence had squeezed the very lifeblood from her veins. Somehow he had taken away from her the ability to nourish her ravenous appetite for life. As she helped to nurse him through his long, last appalling illness she must already have known that her hopes of liberation, of spiritual release, centered upon his death.

Since Julia's death in 1895, the family tie between the Steven's children and the Duckworth's, who Julia brought from her first marriage became lose, though not totally break up until Leslie's death in 1904. In 1900, George Duckworth had inherited a private income. Then he spent money on his half sisters, Vanessa and Virginia. He bought them jewelry and took them to social gatherings which he favorites. Virginia was too shy to enjoy those parties. Beside the torture of the party, Virginia had even suffered from George's disturbing conduct, which was unveiled over 20 years later by herself to the Memoir Club consisted with a group of close family and friends.

Patriarchal oppression from her farther and half brother gave Virginia an early taste of the inferior positions of women and also directed her to the road of struggling for women's rights. After Leslie's death in February 1904, Virginia suffered from the most serious mental breakdown. A series of blows from the deaths of her closest ones—her mother, her half-sister and her farther, brought her headaches. She began to speak incoherently, and then she fell to sense the reality of her surroundings. She was taken charge by a friend of her farther, who was a specialist in mental disorders, and had to be taken care of by three nurses. Following Leslie's death, the Stephens and the Duckworths parted. Vanessa found a house at 46 Gordon Square in Bloomsbury. Virginia joined her after she recovered a little from mental disorder. Thoby and many of his Cambridge friends also came to live in Bloomsbury.

1.2 Her Life in Bloomsbury

At the house in Bloomsbury, Thoby invited his Cambridge friends home to initiate a weekly evening gathering, which was initially called "Thursday Evenings". Wearing informal clothes, they talked whatever they thought mattered. Initially, Virginia listened to their discussions, soon she was attracted by their brilliance and couldn't help becoming a member. During that time, the members of the Bloomsbury Group included art critic Clive Bell, who later became Vanessa's husband; Walter Lamb, secretary of the Royal Academy; literary journalist Desmond Maccarthy; biographer and essayist, Lytton Strachey; civil servant Saxon Sydney Turner; politician Edward Hilton Young; and Leonard Woolf, who later became Virginia's husband. The free cultural atmosphere of the group made Virginia felt at ease to express herself as a woman. As she said in *Moments of Being*, the young men she had named had no "manners" in the Hyde Park Gate sense. They criticized her arguments as severe as their own. They never seemed to notice how she was dressed if she was nice looking or not. So it was in this free cultural atmosphere that Virginia got her wings for her career. Virginia began writing reviews for journals such as *The Guardian* [3], *The Times Literature Supplement* [4] and the *Cornhill Magazine* [5] which won her a small income. She also started to write fiction though not be published until more than fifty years after her death. She also taught drawing, Greek and Latin in Money College. At the same time, she spared much time for reading, translating and wrote descriptive, imaginative and fantastical works, just for her own pleasure. During this period, she finished her first novel "Melymbrosia", which later published as *The Voyage Out*.

It was the free cultural atmosphere of the group that directed Woolf to the path of writing. Together with these close members, her dress and looking which were the old standards were neglected, and she could devote herself whole-heartedly to her beloved career of writing. For all the bitter patriarchal oppressions from her farther and half brother she experienced at an early age, and for all the oppression she saw her farther had placed on her mother and how the later one worn out, Woolf finally found a way to express. According to Woolf's memories, her most vivid childhood memories were not of London but of St. Ives in Cornwall[6], where the family spent every summer until 1895. The Stephens' summer home, Talland House, looked out over Porthminster Bay, and is still standing today, though somewhat altered. Memories of these family holidays and impressions of the landscape, especially the Godrevy Lighthouse, informed the fiction Woolf wrote in later years, most notably *To the Lighthouse*. And she once admitted that her own parents were the prototypes of Mr. and Mrs. Ramsay in her novel *To the Lighthouse*.

Thanks for the education she received at home and the writing practices since she was 9, Woolf soon became a productive author. The 1920's could be a harvest age for Woolf, and it proved that her writing was getting mature with the publication of *A Room of One's Own* in 1929. Besides that, three masterpieces of hers published at the same age could not be neglected. They are *Mrs. Dalloway*, published in 1923, *To the Lighthouse* in 1927 and *Orlando* in 1928. The sudden death of her mother in 1895, when Virginia was 13, and that of her half-sister Stella two years later. She was, however, able to take courses of study (some at degree level) in Greek, Latin, German and history at the Ladies' Department of King's College London[7] between 1897 and 1901, and this brought her into contact with some of the early reformers of women's higher education such as Clara Pater, George Warr and Lilian Faithful.[8] Her sister Vanessa also studied Latin, Italian, art and architecture at King's Ladies' Department. The death of her father in 1904 provoked her most alarming collapse and she was briefly institutionalized. Modern scholars (including her nephew and

biographer, Quentin Bell) have suggested her breakdowns and subsequent recurring depressive periods were also influenced by the sexual abuse to which she and her sister Vanessa were subjected by their half-brothers George and Gerald Duckworth (which Woolf recalls in her autobiographical essays *A Sketch of the Past* and *22 Hyde Park Gate*).

After the death of their father and Virginia's second nervous breakdown, Vanessa and Adrian sold *22 Hyde Park Gate* and bought a house at 46 Gordon Square in Bloomsbury. Woolf came to know the intellectual circle of writers and artists known as the Bloomsbury Group. Several members of the group attained notoriety in 1910 with the Dreadnought hoax, which Virginia participated in disguised as a male Abyssinian royal.[9] Her complete 1940 talk on the Hoax was discovered and is published in the memoirs collected in the expanded edition of *The Platform of Time* (2008). In 1907 Vanessa married Clive Bell, and the couple's interest in avant garden art would have an important influence on Woolf's development as an author. Virginia Woolf married writer Leonard Woolf in 1912, despite his low material status.

1.3 Her Life of Writing

Woolf is a creative writer. Her writing includes novels, book reviews, biographical and autobiographical sketches social and literary criticism, and so on. She is a pioneer of the stream of consciousness technique. Her most famous novels include *Mrs. Dalloway*, *To the Lighthouse*, *Jacob's Room* and *The Waves*. Woolf breaks the traditional creative methods of stream of consciousness and she emphasizes the character's inner-heart rather than the landscape around them.

As all excellent female modernist writer, Virginia Woolf is one of the most prominent writers in English literature feminist and she contributes a lot to feminism. Her life style and works embody her feminism attitudes. During her lifetime, she wrote nine novels, two non-fiction books, a biography and many critical essays and short stories. Virginia Woolf was one of the greatest feminism writers who portrayed the impact of the patriarchal English society on women's lives, the loneliness and frustration of women's lives that had been shaped by the moral, ideological and conventional factors. Many of her works reflected her philosophy of life and identification of women. She grew up with an intense interest in the feminist question, and her novels held the key to the meaning of life and the position of women in the existing patriarchal society. For example: *A Room of One's Own*, *Mrs. Dalloway* and *To the Lighthouse*. Virginia Woolf emphasizes the female should attack the political system of patriarchy society, challenge their traditional ideology and culture with their courage and pursuit the equal rights. Faced with the survival of women in a male-centered society, Virginia Woolf began to think of the question of how to help women to get rid of this kind of problem. They had to improve themselves from various aspects, so they could live independently. To pursue their happiness, they had to strive to overcome all difficulties. Woolf began writing professionally in 1900, initially for the *Times Literary Supplement* with a journalistic piece about Haworth, home of the Bronte family.

Her first novel, *The Voyage Out*, was published in 1915 by her half-brother's imprint, Gerald Duckworth and Company Ltd. This novel was originally entitled *Melymbrosia*, but Woolf repeatedly changed the draft. An earlier version of *The Voyage Out* has been reconstructed by Woolf scholar Louise Desalvo and is now available to the public under the intended title. Woolf went on to publish novels and essays as a public intellectual to both critical and popular success. Much of her work was self-published through the Hogarth Press.[10] She has been hailed as one of the greatest novelists of the twentieth century and one of the foremost modernists. Woolf is considered one of the greatest innovators in the English language. In her works she experimented with stream of consciousness and the underlying psychological as well as emotional motives of characters. Woolf's reputation declined sharply after World War II, but her eminence was reestablished with the surge of feminist criticism in the 1970s.

Her work was criticized for epitomizing the narrow world of the upper-middle class English intelligentsia. Some critics judged it to be lacking in universality and depth, without the power to communicate anything of emotional or ethical relevance to the disillusioned common reader, weary of the 1920s aesthetes. She was also criticized by some as an anti-semite, despite her being happily married to a Jewish man. Virginia Woolf's peculiarities as a fiction writer have tended to obscure her central strength: Woolf is arguably the major lyrical novelist in the English language. Her novels are highly experimental: a narrative, frequently uneventful and commonplace, is refracted—and sometimes almost dissolved—in the characters' receptive consciousness. Intense lyricism and stylistic virtuosity fuse to create a world overabundant with auditory and visual impressions. The intensity of Virginia Woolf's poetic vision elevates the ordinary, sometimes banal settings-often wartime environments-of most of her novels. For example, *Mrs Dalloway* (1925) centres on the efforts of Clarissa Dalloway, a middle-aged society woman, to organize a party, even as her life is paralleled with that of Septimus Warren Smith, a working-class veteran who has returned from the World War Ⅰ bearing deep psychological scars.

To the Lighthouse (1927) is set on two days ten years apart. The plot centers around the Ramsay family's anticipation of and reflection upon a visit to a lighthouse and the connected familial tensions. One of the primary themes of the novel is the struggle in the creative process that beset painter Lily Briscoe while she struggles to paint in the midst of the family drama. The novel is also a Lytton Strachey and Woolf at Garsington, 1923. It also explores the passage of time, and how women are forced by society to allow men to take emotional strength from them.

Orlando (1928) has a different quality from all Virginia Woolf's other novels suggested by its subtitle, "A Biography", as it attempts to represent the character of a real person and is dedicated to Vita Sackville-West. It was meant to console Vita for being a girl and for the loss of her ancestral home, though it is also a satirical treatment of Vita and her work. In Orlando, the techniques of historical biographers are being ridiculed; the character of a pompous biographer is being assumed in order for it to be mocked.

The Waves (1931) presents a group of six friends whose reflections, which are closer to recitatives than to interior monologues proper, create a wave-like atmosphere that is more akin to a prose poem than to a plot-centered novel. Her last work, *Between the Acts* (1941) sums up and magnifies Woolf's chief preoccupations: the transformation of life through art, sexual ambivalence, and meditation on the themes of flux of time and life, presented simultaneously as corrosion and rejuvenation—all set in a highly imaginative and symbolic narrative encompassing almost all of English history. This book is the most lyrical of all her works, not only in feeling but in style being chiefly written in verse.

While nowhere near a simple recapitulation of the coterie's ideals, Woolf's work can be understood as consistently in dialogue with Bloomsbury, particularly its tendency (informed by G. E. Moore, among others) towards doctrinaire rationalism. Her works have been translated into over 50 languages, by writers of the calibre of Jorge Luis Borges and Marguerite Your cenar. So woolf is well-known in China even the world, as one of most famous and successful female writers, and her contribution to the world literature history is significant.

Notes

1. Bloomsbury is a cultural group, which was set up in 1905 in segpan'house with Woolf and her sister Vanessa as the hostesses. Its members includeed Cambridge elites, such as the biographer and essayist Lytton Strachey (1880-1932), the classics scholar and musician Sydney-Turchey (1880-1962), and the critic Clive Bell (1881-1964), the group was neither an organization nor self-consciously a movement, still less a political party, it had no manifesto, notwithstanding at least one attempt to claim art as a platform for the group cause.

2. Hyde Park Gate is an apartment set in London, 300m from Royal Albert Hall, 1.2 km from Hyde Park.

3. *The Guardian* is a British daily newspaper, known from 1821 until 1959 as *The Manchester Guardian*. Along with its sister papers *The Observer* and *The Guardian Weekly*, *The Guardian* is part of the Guardian Media Group, owned by The Scott Trust Limited.

4. *The Times Literature Supplement* first appeared in 1902 as a supplement to *The Times*, but became a separate publication in 1914. Many distinguished writers have been contributors, including T. S. Eliot, Henry James, and Virginia Woolf, but now it is the leading international weekly for literary culture.

5. *The Cornhill Magazine* (1860-1975) was a Victorian magazine and literary journal named after the publisher's address at 65 Cornhill in London.

6. St Ives is the town of coastline which takes its name from St Ia, the daughter of an Irish chieftain, who is said to have sailed to Cornwall in the mid 5th Century on a leaf, having missed the boat carrying other saints. Its Cornish name is Porthia ("Ia's cove") and its pre-Christian name is believed to be Pendennis ("headland fort"). St Ives built its prosperity on pilchard fishing and the trade in Cornish slate and minerals. In 1770 John Smeaton built the Eddystone lighthouse, with the arrival of the railway in 1877 and the growth of mass tourism soon turned St Ives into a

popular holiday resort. Where Woolf often spent her childhood like the stories in *To the Lighthouse.*

7. *King's College* was established in 1896, the founder and principal, Mr Graham Bruce, described the aim of the College as being able to provide "the best all-round education it is possible to obtain".

8. Clara Pater, George Warr and Lilian Faithful are Principal of the King's Ladies' Department and noted as one of the Steamboat ladies.

9. The Dreadnought hoax was a practical joke pulled by Horace de Vere Cole in 1910. Cole tricked the Royal Navy into showing their flagship, the battleship HMS Dreadnought, to a fake delegation of Abyssinian royals. The hoax drew attention in Britain to the emergence of the Bloomsbury Group, among whom some of Cole's collaborators numbered. The hoax was a repeat of a similar impersonation which Cole and Adrian Stephen had organised while they were students at Cambridge in 1905.

10. The Hogarth Press was a British publishing house founded in 1917 by Leonard Woolf and Virginia Woolf. It was named after their house in Richmond, in which they began hand-printing books. The press was fiestly set up in the dining room of Hogarth House, where the Woolfs lived, lending its name to the publishing company they founded.

Chapter Two The Overall Study on Virginia Woolf Abroad and Home Recently

Woolf's studies began at the time she was alive and have continued to be trendy until present. J. Goldman divides Woolf studies into the following stages: from 1910s to 1940s, studies focused on her reform and experiment on novels and the impact of impressionism; during 1950s to 1960s, scholars studied from the perspectives of philosophy, psychology and mythology; in 1970s, with the rising of feminist movement, scholars paid much attention to Woolf's feminist thoughts, especially her androgynous theory, modernism and her aesthetic ideology; in 1980s, feminist studies of Woolf continued to develop and post-modernist studies flourished; from 1990s to present, Woolf's studies take on new look and touch various aspects including feminism, historism, post-colonialism and ethnics. From Goldman's categorization, the trend of Woolf's studies is closely related to the development of literary thoughts and culture movements with the times, and these stages of Woolf's studies are not cut off but interrelated with each other. The following list part of the noticeable studies on Virginia Woolf and her works.

In *The Novels of Virginia Woolf* (1977), Mitchell Alexander Leaska studies Woolf's several novels including *To the Lighthouse* in which he argues that the novel is a dramatic realistic, ironic story of a family life; the sexual antitheses of the Ramsay couple are emphasized and satirized; the constant emphasis on the disparity between thought and action of the characters is to show the difficulty of infusing shapes with sense; the universal inhibition of characters intends to reveal the intricate relationship between the external environment and the inner meanings.

With the development in psychology and psychiatry, many critics studied Virginia Woolf and her works from the psycho-biographical perspective after the 1980s. Lyndall Gordon makes a meditative and thematic biography of Virginia Woolf by combining her works with her private life: her memories of childhood, the odd education, the volcanic madness and the unusual marriage. James King's Virginia Woolf (1994) develops Cordon's tradition and treats more leisurely on Woolf's marriage, friendships, mental instability and sexuality to interpret the great author's life. In *The Flight of the Mind*—Virginia Woolf's Art mid *Manic-Depressive Illness* (1992), Thomas C. Caramagno argues that Virginia Woolf's symptoms fulfill the manic-depressive paradigm and he applies psychiatric theory to study Woolf's novels to show how the epistemological difficulties are intimately bound up with Woolf's manic-depressive illness. Her novels dramatize her struggle to establish a bipolar sense of identity. In assuming the role of mediator between fictionalized representatives of her family and of her seemingly bifurcated self, Woolf discovers the power and self-confidence that insight and creativity bring to artist. In *The Unknown Virginia Woolf* (1995), Roger Poole also relates Woolf's works to her life and argued that Woolf doesn't aim to solve the conflicts in her novels; her characters only become the embodiments through which she exorcises herself and her parents, so as to exorcise her mental illness and painful conflicts of consciousness in her mind, and therefore gain peacefulness and freedom.

From the 1990s to this day, as literary criticism become more dynamic and diversified, scholars also study Virginia Woolf and her works from various perspectives. In "Virginia Woolf and Modernism", Michael Whitworth discusses the modernist characteristics of Virginia Woolf's works and argues that the strand of late-Victorian aestheticism in Woolf's modernist thinking keeps her at a critical distance from the aesthetic preferences of many of her modernist contemporaries; she maintains a critical distance from the polities which corresponds to the metaphors, a politics of authoritarianism and exaggerated masculinity; and this divergence is influenced by her immediate literary community and her political outlook. In "The Impact of Post-impressionism", Sue Roe studies the post-impressionist impact on Virginia Woolf's writing. She argues that Woolf's language and style are essentially expressionist and owes her expressionist ideas to her living environment and her involvement in the Bloomsbury circle; inspired by the post-impressionists, Virginia Woolf is courageous to break the traditional writing rules and depict a vision of simultaneity within the human psyche through a visual medium. In "Virginia Woolf and the Language of Authorship", Maria Dibattista probes into the meaning of silence in Woolf's works. She argues that silence is a language of interiors which represents the hidden unexpressed life of women who have sat indoors for thousands of years; Virginia Woolf in her works presents us an art by contemplating the unheard voice to approach the disassociated state of consciousness akin to autism. And in "Woolf's Feminism and Feminism's Woolf", Laura Marias makes a general review of Virginia Woolf's feminist ideas and the feminist criticism on Woolf and her works. Laura cites Woolf's fable of Shakespeare's sister to illustrate her ideas on "silence". According to Laura, the story resonates with the feminist model of women's silence, the burial and repression of their gifts, and a literary history in which women's absence becomes constructed as a speaking silence. The negative absence underlies a powerful strength which would support the modern women to seek for the way to be independent. *In Virginia Woolf and the Visible World* (2001), Emily Dalgarno studies the changes of the conception of beauty in Woolf's works. She points out that "beauty" is a master signaler and is deconstructed by Woolf; "beauty" is a fixed term that represents the ideology of gender. In *To the Lighthouse*, Mrs. Ramsay is given frequent and unvarying emphasis of her beauty. Beauty is repeated over and over by the male characters in a gesture that praises while it often belittles Mrs. Ramsay; Beauty, when associated with the male gaze, is unanimated and freezes life; for Lily Briscoe, beauty is an obstacle which prevents her from integrating her aesthetic theory with the practice of painting. Only when Lily is able to sequester herself from the male discourse she redefines the term "beauty" as a speech act which permits her to complete her work.

In "Virginia Woolf Studies in China in the Late 20 Years", scholars Gao Fen and Lu Yan give a general review of Woolf's studies in China from various aspects including translation and publication, general study and text analysis. According to their study, in China the translation and introduction of Virginia Woolf's works began as early as 1930s. However, a comprehensive study did not start until the 1980s. And the domestic studies mainly focus on three aspects: Woolf's theory of novel writing, Woolf's writing practice and Woolf's feminist literary criticism.

In 1982, Qu Shijing published "Woolf's to the Lighthouse" in *Foreign Literature Reports*, which introduced and analyzed Virginia Woolf and her novel for the first time. He pointed that the theme of the novel was exploring the meaning of life and the essence of oneself. And in 1989 Qu Shijing published his monograph: Virginia Woolf, the Novelist of Stream of Consciousness in which he first introduced Woolf's writing technique Stream-of-Consciousness. Qu's study of Woolf paved the way for the scholars afterward. For example, in "Time Aesthetics of *To the Lighthouse* by Virginia Woolf", Lu Jing studies the narration time of the novel which she thinks to deal with the relation between clock time and psychological time, the work adopts a time structure of concentric circles in narration, manifested by a frequent alternation between time of narration and time of flowing consciousness. Another scholar Lv Hongling also makes thorough study of Woolf's practice of writing. In her *Emotion & Reason: A Study of Virginia Woolf's Conception of Women's Writing* (2004), Lv argues that the issue of emotion and reason is the core of Woolf's writings and theoretical thinking about women's writing; the union of emotion and reason is possible in the pursuit of poetic spirit by impersonality, and that the woman writer should develop a consciousness of reasoned emotion for the full exertion of her creativity. In "On the Poetic Quality of Virginia Woolf's Writing", Yuan Jingyu indicates that the poetic quality of Woolf's works originates in her realization of the importance of poeticized fiction, her choice of literary tradition, the changes of her day as well as her feminist stance; the features of symbol, music and painting demonstrated in her major novels are her unique contribution to the aestheticism of modern fiction.

Feminist studies of Virginia Woolf and her works began in late 1990s in China and later were focused on her androgynous theory and her feminine standpoints. For example, Shu Yongzhen applies the contemporary feminist theories to study Woolf's novel *To the Lighthouse* which she considers as Woolf's conscious fulfillment of her feminist thinking. Guo Hangna and Wang Wen study Woolf's literary theory on women writing especially her "a room of one's own", which they define as "a private space essential for women writing"; and they argue that the material and spiritual pressures and difficulties writing women come across in their literary creation form the basis for Woolf to build her theories in feminine literary criticism. They also make a feminist study of Woolf's novel *To the Lighthouse* and indicate that the compromise or intermediacy between reason and emotion is an ideal way of feminist expression. Wu Qinghong argues in her essay "On Virginia Woolf's Feminist Ideas" that "Virginia Woolf criticized the political, economic and cultural systems of the patriarchal society and proposed to reexamine the human history from the female angle with a view to creating a new civilization". And in her *Virginia Woolf and Feminism* (2005) Wu makes an extensional study on Woolf's relationship with the feminist movement. Many other scholars have made related studies, for instance, Cai Fang and Xie

Baohui exemplified Woolf's novel *Orlando* to study the androgynous personality of *Orlando* based on Woolf's poetics theory of androgyny; Xiao Ping and Fang Yonglan study Woolf's feminist stand by adopting Susan S. Lancer's theory on feminist narratology. Also Yu Li in her "Beautiful Illusion Dissolved in Voice—Listening the Voice of Woolf's *To the Lighthouse*" studies the voice and beauty of the female images especially Mrs. Ramsay from the perspective of feminist narration. There are also some scholars who make comparative study between Woolf and other feminists, like Wang Lili's "Seeking for Mother's Memory: A Comparison between Woolf and Lessing" which displays the similarities and differences between the two great feminist icons. These studies show that Woolf's feminist ideas have made great influence and continue to draw scholars' attention in the field of literary criticism.

Still a lot of scholars study Virginia Woolf and her works from other perspectives. For example, He Yahui in her "On Virginia Woolf's Tragic Sense" points out that Virginia Woolf's sense of death and lack of interpersonal understanding and horror of the war yield her tragic sense shown as personal sadness, puzzle and perplexity; however, her choice of suicide shows "the transcendence of man's principal spirit over the tragedy rather than the sadness of human life". Also in "Death and Change: Connotations of Virginia Woolf's Mrs Dalloway, *To the Lighthouse* and *The Waves*", Du Juan also probes into the death consciousness in Woolf's novels and highlights her transcendence over life and death. In "Ecological Selfhood by Double Deconstruction of Logo-centrism", Li Aiyun expounds Virginia Woolf's ecoconsciousness and eco-wisdom by studying her *Jacob's Room* in which Li thinks Woolf "deconstructs androcentrism through the illusion of Jacob, and mancentrism by man-naturalization and natural humanization, thus transcending the bounds of Logos-centrism". And in "The Image of the UK Empire in Virginia Woolf's Novels", Xie Jiangnan argues that the image of the UK Empire played an important role in Woolf's novels in which she "described and represented the historical situation in the decay of the Empire objectively including its diminished power and floundering struggle". Anyway, with the nourishment of literary criticism, abroad and domestic studies of Virginia Woolf are developing fast and have made contribution to the worldwide studies of Virginia Woolf.

Chapter Three Her Feminist Ideas

3.1 The Development of Feminist Movement in Britain

Under the influence of the Enlightenment,[1] feminism came in Britain at the end of the 18th century and formed a political trend. It came to its climax at the turn of the 20th century, which was called the First Feminism Wave. Mary Wollstonecraf (1759–1797) thought out her *A Vindication of the Rights of Woman* (1792), in which she considered better education and reform of the law to be the way to improve woman's situation at the end of that century. This book inherited a legacy of the Enlightenment—the vocabulary of "the rights of man", with which feminists were to demand rights for women, and which was regarded as the founding text of modern feminism.

The early stage of women's movement was integrated with political movements such as the French Revolution of 1789, the Chartism Movement[2] in Britain and the anti-slavery movement in the US for human rights on the whole; however, those movements were preoccupied essentially with manhood, and women's depressed situation as half the population and the second sex were even ignored by their male comrades. As time came to the latter half of the 19th century, the strongest women's movement in Europe emerged in the United Kingdom. Women started to demand votes. Their arguments rested on the principle of natural rights: if men had such a right, it could not be in justice to be denied to women. In 1870, the Married Women's Property Act was passed, which allowed British women to own property and in the same year, British women were given the right to vote in local elections after a long and arduous struggle. However, the convention believing women and their property belonged to their husbands was deep-rooted among people. Women in real life still had hard time to practice their rights. Not until 1918 were women given the full rights of voting in the UK.

Feminism is generally accepted as a movement and theory concerned with advancing the position of women through such means as achievement of political, legal, or economic rights equal to those granted men. Modern feminism was an offshoot of the Enlightenment, the vast movement of ideas among European intellectuals in the eighteenth century, which was characterized by attacks on conventional beliefs and by unlimited faith in the perfectibility of mankind through the application of reason to human affairs. In this movement, some philosophers started to cast doubt on the accepted subordination of women and advocate women's rights as part of "the rights of man".

The word "feminism" was not in general usage till the 1890s and it was in the late 19th century that feminist movements finally established themselves as significant and permanent features of the European political landscape. Feminism helped undoubtedly to alter the modes of thought and of life of women from all classes in the 19th century. During the two world wars in the 20th century, women got respect from their male partners because of their ability in their professions. After the World War Ⅱ, with many soldiers returning home, women were driven back home to play their feminine roles. The change after a period of successful performance in career made them uneasy and dissatisfaction and doubt in their status were intensified with the outbreak of the Civil Rights Movement[3] in the US. Thus formed the Second Feminism Wave.[4] This time, women started to cast suspicion on the dominant ideology which could easily change what they had got. They traced women's disadvantageous situation back to the very root: the patriarchy, and launched a movement in a far broader sense.

Feminist criticism since it took its shape in the 1960s has attracted much attention from researchers in favor of women's interests. Women's study thus became an important current in the present academies. But to understand the principles or features of feminist criticism, we shall not shun studying "feminism", which has direct connection with the formation of feminist criticism.

Feminism has been and remains today, a political challenge to male authority and hierarchy in the most profound sense. And moreover, because of the non-violence characteristic of feminism, it is easily led to a cultural criticism. It is not only a series of women's movements, but formed an ideology for sociopolitical changes based on a critical analysis of male privilege and women's subordination within any given society. Therefore, the ultimate vision of feminism was "transformational".

Based on this understanding of feminism, a feminist can be considered any person, female or male, whose ideas and actions show them to meet at least three criteria: Firstly, they recognize the validity of women's own interpretations of their lived experience and needs and acknowledge the values women claim publicly as their own (as distinct from an aesthetic ideal of womanhood invented by men) in assessing their status in society relative to men; Secondly, they exhibit consciousness of, discomfort at, or even anger over institutionalized injustice toward women as a group by men as a group in a men's society; Thirdly, they advocate the elimination of that injustice by challenging through efforts to alter prevailing ideas or social institutions and practices, the coercive power, force, or authority that upholds male prerogatives in that particular culture. Feminist criticism coming into being in the 1960s integrated the "transformational" spirit of feminism with literary criticism, trying to raise women's self consciousness and their potentialities to oppose the patriarchy and women's subordination. Feminist critics tried to find evidence in literature that was dominated by males for women's oppression and silence, focusing their attention to rewrite about women's exclusive experience that had never been positively represented in male literature. Thus, many women writers were dug out of anonymity and the ever much studied women writers were researched in a new perspective.

The tradition of female writing in British literature has a long history and the real sense of female literature in England began in the 19th century Victorian era. Jane Austen's works reflect the preliminary awakening of female consciousness; in the creation of the Bronte sisters' the strong anti – consciousness and the sense of economic independence get fully demonstrated; In Mrs. Gaskell's[5] works, the female consciousness has risen to ethics and psychological level and image to show women's inner confusion and thinking. The female writers who were discriminated against in Victoria in nineteenth century, the female writers' awakening of female consciousness can be seen from the following three aspects.

Firstly, the fight for language discourse right. In the nineteenth century, Britain is the traditional patriarchal society, as the angle at home, women were confined to the family, women's discourse power is completely deprived, leading to the loss of the independent consciousness of women in 1847. The publication of *Jane Eyre*[6] shed the first light for the female consciousness. Jane has full consciousness to the importance of the right to speak, and the same equality. For example when Jane Eyre in Thornfield Hall, facing the arrogant pride master, she did not bow and scrape effusive. In order to get the freedom and equality of love, Jane loudly declared: her soul was like him as well as her heart. They stand before God's heels on the heels of equality because they are equal. She married him, rather than he married her.

Next, the affirmation of women's intelligence. For women in the United Kingdom of Victoria[7] in the period of the nineteenth century, compared with men, it is generally believed that women are less intelligent than men. The vast majority of women also recognized this concept. They have no sense of their own humble status. Jane Austen's works have fully affirmed the intelligence of women, and she thinks that women's intelligence is the same as men's intelligence. Men and women are the same. Both have the advantages and disadvantages. Elizabeth, the heroine of *Pride and Prejudice*, has a strong sense of humor. She is no less intelligent than any one of the men in the novel.

Finally, the establishment of the female identity. Jane Austen's female consciousness is also reflected in her identification of the female identity of the novel *Pride and Prejudice*. The heroine Elizabeth is an extraordinary woman of publicity of the anti-traditional personality. She is a pursuit of independence and dignity of women to fight for their own love. The strong feminine consciousness, which is shown by the dignity of the women, opens up a new chapter in the history of English literature. Elizabeth Gaskell considered as one of the outstanding novelist wrote many short stories, such as *Mary Barton*[8], *Cranford* and *His Wife and Children*. These works reflects the works of England in the 19th century in the period of social transformation caused by many changes and conflict. Gus Kyle lady describes a group of women gradually moving toward the field of society, on the basis of Jane Austen and Bronte sisters' exploration, she put the female consciousness into the orbit of society, and also displayed female participation in social activities and their ability and quality in the social and political fields. So Mrs. Gaskell was advocated as women's action ability of the pioneer.

3.2 The Development of Woolf's Feminist Ideas

3.2.1 The Familiy Background

Virginia Woolf was not only a famous critic, essayist, novelist, and biographer, but also a prominent precursor of modern feminist literary criticism of the twentieth century. She was born at Hyde Park Gate in 1882, the little daughter of the eminent editor and critic, Sir Leslie Stephen, and his wife Julia Jackson Duckworth. She grew up in a cultured and literary atmosphere, receiving her education from the tutor and her father's extensive library, while her brothers were sent to the public schools and then to Cambridge to receive the best education. Virginia Woolf was extremely conscious of the disadvantages of not being well educated. After the death of her father, Virginia Woolf suffered the first major breakdown in 1904. Afterwards she settled in the Bloomsbury district of London with her brother Thoby and sister Vanessa, and soon she became a central figure of the Bloomsbury Group, where she met Leonard Woolf, who later became her husband in 1912.

Woolf, who has been constantly considered as a talented female novelist and modern theoretical master, has an unhappy childhood. She perhaps is not a thorough feminist, but she is quite conscious of feminism. Virginia Woolf's female sensibilities are derived from her own experiences as being a female in the male-dominated Victorian society as well as from her observation of the experiences and her conception of the situation of the female figures around her. The sufferings she had as being a female (for example, she had been molested by her two half brothers) and the sufferings of female figures around her made her seek the cause for the inevitable tragic fate of women and seek a solution for women's liberation through her literary works. It is the Victorian family pattern and the ideology that leads to the tragic ending of women, especially daughters, in the Victorian family. In Leslie Stephen's, because of the social pressure, Leslie Stephen is worried about failure all the time. He is a typical egocentric man with strong patriarchal style in Victorian Age. However, Julia Duckworth who could no longer bear the oppression not only from society but also from her large family, eventually dies from the comprehensive stress in 1895. After the death of Julia, Leslie turns to Stella. On one hand, she has to console her stepfather; on the other hand, she must satisfy his requirements. However, under her mother's influence, Stella regards it as her inevitable duty. After she is married to Jack Hill, Stella [9] is seriously ill, and dies of Peritonitis at last. What happens to Laura Stephen [10] can be understood as the tragic outcome of that ideology of Victorian children who does not act correctly, mind their manners, and who refuses the control of the parents. She is considered to be evil and deserved harsh punishments. Rebel against the punishments is a challenge to the family authority and a threat to the patriarchal family institution. This is the case for Laura: she is a child engaging in bad behavior, but she does not welcome punishment. She reacts against it as if it is unwarranted. As a result, Laura is treated as a non being, a non person within the Stephen household. Though living in the same home with her family, she is put away in a different part of the house from the rest of the family. She lives throughout Virginia Woolf's childhood, but she ceases to exist, in any real sense, as far as the family is concerned. She is the very own mad woman in the attic in the Stephen family. Stella, in this sense, is a victim of the ideology of the role of daughter that Julia trains her to hold to. She is submissive and defenseless. She is suffering in the course of meeting her step-father's living as well as emotional needs. She is unhappy in her expressions of the female sensibilities. So Woolf examines the female sufferings around her and the conclusion she made from her conception of the female sufferings.

As a female writer, Virginia Woolf is very angry at the unequal treatment between male and female. Taking the family of Leslie Stephen for example, the two brothers are entitled to the famous university to accept the best education even if they do bad in study. On the contrary, the pretty and industrious sisters, who are eager to receive more education, are confined to stay at home. In a letter to her brother, Virginia Woolf expresses the strong feeling directly and anxiously. In many of her literary works, she demands the right of education for women in the patriarchal society. Unfortunately, Woolf gets sexual abuse from her two half brothers in her childhood because of her parents' negligence. This makes Woolf from her deep heart feel that women are maltreated by men. A strong sense of anti-patriarchy comes into her mind. Based on her own experience, Woolf, like many other early feminists thinks that there is no difference between women and men by nature. In her opinion, it is different education that makes distance between women and men. Laura is sent to the asylum and lives all her lonely life there; Stella suffers from the overburden housework and died early. After Julia's death, Woolf and her two sisters are left with no defense at all, fully exposed to the male's brutality and lust. Being brought up in such a family institution that maintains the superiority of men and the inferiority of women, it is not strange for Virginia Woolf to develop so acute insights about the situation of women as reveals in her novels. By deciding to become a writer, Virginia Woolf is not violating her parents' expectations of the gender-determined proper roles for males and females. She will, however, use her art in ways that challenges traditional beliefs about men and women. Hence, we find her expression of female sensibilities scatter through nearly all of her major works.

3.2.2 The Social Background

It is true that the female experiences she has conceived has a great influence on her writing about women, and it is acknowledged that the source of any thought can not do without the social background. So one of the sources of Virginia Woolf's unique female consciousness comes from the social environment at that time. In British history, there are several Women's Liberation Movements, in which women strive for the equal rights with men. These rights cover many aspects, such as politics, economy, writing, education and so on. After the struggles, Women's liberation movements makes great progress, and women earn some rights. For instance, in 1870, English women win the right of property; in 1919, English women are allowed to run for Parliament; and in 1928, they win the right to vote. Thanks to the strong force of Women's Liberation Movement, many women begin to wake up. After winning the rights in politics, they demand to have the equal rights with men in literature. Such requirements also provide unique weapons of thought for Women's Liberation Movements, which propel the development of women's movements forcefully.

Woolf advocates that women should have equal rights with men in politics, economics and legislation. She wrote, "Independence is the first need for women." [11] Only when women get economic independence can they realize self and further push emancipation from all aspects. She, then, on abolishment of restriction to women's employment which exerted by British Parliament, highly appraised, "The doors suddenly open. Every woman can have a new penny in her wallet. Thanks to it, each mind, eyesight and action represents a new idea." [12] On the other hand, Virginia Woolf also perceives the harm of the traditional patriarchal culture from her own mother Julia Duckworth and her two half sisters Laura and Stella. Women in Victorian are educated to be docile, amicable and submissive. They are expected to be "the Angels in the House". Julia Duckworth, a typical Victorian fair lady, takes care of her large family without any complaints. Under that situation, Woolf had a clear feminist consciousness.

3.3 Virginia Woolf ' s Feminist Ideas

Woolf was much concerned with the position of women, especially professional women, and the constrictions they suffered under. She wrote several cogent essays on the subject, notably in *A Room of One's Own* and *Three Guines*. These works embody her unique female consciousness and advanced feminist idea. Hence, she was regarded as the important precursor of modern feminist literary criticism.

In *A Room of One's Own*, Virginia Woolf put foreword her own point of view as following: firstly, Woolf observed that having a private room in which to think and write is a basic requirement for producing literature, a requirement that, along with economic independence, few women in history had ever enjoyed. Raising the question of why women had not produced much first-rate fiction, Woolf described the poverty, social pressures, family demands, and lack of education that tended to prevent women from writing. "A woman must have money and a room of her own if she is to write fiction." This sentence was perhaps the most famous line from this essay. In other words, women must strive for financial, social and psychological independence. She used the room as a symbol for many larger issues, such as privacy, leisure time, and financial independence, each of which was an essential component of the countless inequalities between men and women. Virginia Woolf has written a great deal of works about women's writing, and she continually examines the problems facing women writers. With the acute observation, Virginia Woolf indicates the contemporary conditions of women's writing and visualizes the ideal state of women's writing. She believes that women have always faced social and economic obstacles to their literary ambitions. With her industrious work, Virginia Woolf continuously advocates the proposition of women's writing. She hopes to achieve a balance between "male" self-realization and "female" self-annihilation.

In *A Room of One's Own*, Virginia Woolf analyzes the contemporary conditions of women's writing, and discusses the outer conditions and inner state of ideal women's writing. She is confident with the future of women's writing. However, there is still no better writing atmosphere for women. Up to the early nineteenth century, there is only a single sitting room in the middle-class family. Women writers have no separate study for writing. They have to complete their writings in the general sitting room, so she criticizes that patriarchy lulls and restricts people's thoughts and manners.

Secondly, Woolf paid more attention to evaluate the former women writers and their literary history. She thought that all of the great women novelists were based on the numerous forerunners' unremitting endeavors. As Woolf indicated in *A Room of One's Own*:

"Without those forerunners, Jane Austen and the Brontes, George Eliot could no more have written than Shakespeare could have written Marlowe, or Marlowe without those forgotten poets who paved the ways and tamed the natural savagery of the tongue. For masterpieces are not single and solitary births; they are the outcome of many years of thinking in common, of thinking by the body of the people, so that the experience of the mass is behind the single voice. Jane Austen should have laid a wreath upon the grave of Fanny Burney, and George Eliot done homage to the robust shade of Elize Carter-the valiant old woman who tied a bell to her bedstead in order that she might wake early and learn Greek. All women together ought to let flowers fall upon the tomb of Aphra Behn, which is, most scandalously but rather appropriately, in Westminster Abbey, for it was she who earned them the right to speak their minds."[13]

Thirdly, Woolf discussed the relationship between men and women. She argued that they should be equal in society, and endeavored to search for equality between them. From her description, we come to realize that women must obey the will of their parents; otherwise, they would be punished severely. And the sum of money is very important for her, and has changed her life completely. The author held view that the relationship between men and women changed greatly after women had money. Women were not secondary to men, and they are equal at least. They need objective social environment for writing. She pondered over the inner state of women's writing. On the basis of this point, Woolf posed the famous theory of "androgynous vision".

The term androgyny derives from two Greek words andro and gyn, which refer to male and female respectively, and the combination of the two words represents the human impulse to unite male and female into a harmonious one. In Woolf's *A Room of One's Own*, she has set forth her androgyny theory explicitly:

In each of us two powers preside, one male, one female; and in the man's brain, the man predominates over the woman, and in the woman's brain, the woman predominates over the man. The normal and comfortable state of being is that when the two live in harmony together; in a phallocentric society, male and female are in binary opposition. Male are in the center of the society while female are expelled to the edge of it. The only significance of female's existence to male is to prove their higher social standard. In order to protect their patriarchal power, male praise highly this kind of binary opposition which emphasizes male's priority. Deconstructive feminists thoroughly repudiate patriarchal binary opposition, phallocentricism and logocentrism, attempting to shatter patriarchal binary opposition. In a sense, Woolf's androgyny theory follows deconstruct feminism' s suit. What's more, the former one has put forward a final solution.

In *Mrs. Dalloway*, Woolf characterized an image of a new woman—Sally. She is a manly woman who has got most of male's excellent qualities. She has got a rational head; she is not bother about trifles; she is even tough and bold and decisive. She is not rational, and she won't know which kind of life she prefers; she won't appreciate her husband who is the son of a miner, because she is not tough and bold and decisive. She won't make her decision to marry a miner's son and enjoy her happy marriage. Besides, Sally also has the quality of a kind lady. In her marriage, Sally is an understanding wife and a loving mother. Her deep love to the family members and her care for the household enhance the cohesion of the family. Sally's ideal marriage confirms Woolf's conclusion: " A woman also must have intercourse with the man in her...".[13] A counter evidence is presented in *To the Lighthouse*. Woolf has once admitted that the prototype of Mr. and Mrs. Ramsay are her own parents. Her father was a domestic tyranny who greedily demanded his wife's care and psychological support while her mother was a typical Victorian housewife who has devoted her whole life to her husband and her children. A similar story was presented in *To the Lighthouse*. The father's endless demand has worn out the mother. The mother with pure femininity and the father with pure masculine form a sharp binary opposition.

In a phallocentric society, patriarchal power undoubtedly occupies the higher position which oppresses female who is in a weak position. When this kind of oppression accumulates to a certain extent that the other pole of the binary could no longer afford to undertake, the weak pole dies out. Following the death of the weak pole, the binary opposition distinguishes. Without a basis to lie their power and control, the former controller no longer exists. From the opposite side, Woolf makes it clear that "... The normal and comfortable state of being is that when the two (female and male power) live in harmony together, spiritually cooperating...".[13]

Stopping at *To the Lighthouse*, Woolf's androgyny theory could far from being considered to be completed. Though in *To the Lighthouse*, Woolf has put forward that female and male power should live "in harmony together" and "spiritually cooperating", male's duty in contribution to the harmony of this binary opposition had yet to put forward explicitly until the appearance of *Orlando: A Biography*. This novel describes how a male becomes a female and with both power in head, she turns out to be a successful poet. In *Mrs. Dalloway*, Woolf had put forward that women should bear male power in head. This is part of her androgyny theory, but stop here, readers may be confused: Is that to say male's quality is better than female, so that female should adopt it? Is Woolf's theory a kind of compromise to the phallocentric society? The novel *Orlando: A Biography* gives a negative answer. It shows that "... If one is a man, still the woman part of the brain must have effect..." Not until this, readers get a clear view of Woolf's androgyny theory.

From *Mrs. Dalloway* published in 1923, to *To the Lighthouse* published in 1927, and then, to *Orlando: A Biography* which published in 1928, Woolf's theory was improved and perfected, and finally, in 1929, she gave a systematic and complete presentation of the theory in her masterpiece *A Room of One's Own*. Either her emphasis on female's self conscious or a creative head, Woolf's feminism never sentences patriarchal power to death, instead, she insists on that no matter women and men in a biological sense or the female and male power in a man or woman, both sexes should live in coherence and harmony.

Fourthly, Woolf expresses in her works her philosophy of life. She was growing in a background where there were lots of feminist questions, and she shows her identification and opinion on women and seek for life's meaning and female position in her novels. Just like Naik cited in *Aston* (1998) comments: "In her writing,

Woolf makes a sifting appraisal of women's problem, their peculiar dilemmas and conditioning in the traditional Victorian society. Woolf was the most vociferous and vehement on feminist issues such as subjectivity, class, sexuality and culture. In tier critiques, Woolf questions an aesthetic that disallows anger, unreason and passion as productive emotions." In a long period of time, there was dissertation that female works were filled of feelings of fear and anger. However, Woolf does not believe that it was because women writers are not as talented as man, but because women cannot express their real feelings freely at that time and their talents was crippled. Naik cited in *Aston* (1998) remarks: "Woolf felt that novels written by women were influenced by their resentment to the treatment meted on their sex and ended up pleading for their rights. Woolf felt that this weakened the cause of women struggling to carve a niche for themselves in the literary canon." And there is also need for self-organization and change in gender identity-different masculinity and femininity. She thinks that the society do not only serve for men, but also for women. That is to say, there should be a society serve for man and woman life. In that society, both male and female identities are realized. Woolf believed that women have special values that men do not have, such as what was mentioned before that they are peaceful. She believes these unique values are compelling reasons that it's necessary to let women take participation in public life and improve the defective social system. She stressed that education of women will merit our society. She appealed for women to rebuild history and society based on their own values. Obviously, the rebuilt history and society are different from the history and society based on human violence.

Fifthly, Woolf strived to give women female identity. In Woolf's strife to set the woman away from the patriarchal society, she called women to rewrite the history of women through female eyes and talk about themselves and their experiences truthfully. Woolf, in her essay "Professions for Women" suggests that the two main reasons for her to have a professional life as a female writer were "killing the Angel in the House" and "telling the truth about my own experiences as a body". This idea of taking writing as a career not incidentally corresponds to the influence of her family background and the influence of the female literature tradition. Since she is born into a typical Victorian family and sees the sufferings and pains of the female figures in the family all through her life. It is her duty as a woman novelist to expose the women's sufferings and attacks the image of "the Angel in the House" in her novels. Meanwhile, it is expected that education revolution should seek only for knowledge instead of fame, degree, doctrine and pompousness. In order to build up such a beautiful and peaceful world and establish women's female identity, Woolf calls on women to reconstruct society and history in light of their own thoughts and values. It is obvious that the reconstruction should be based on women's spirit and culture rather than men's violence. Woolf advocates that women must make use of ideology to overthrow the patriarchal pattern.

In her eyes, the best way is writing. She deems that it is because of men's long oppression that women lose their rights of speech. Women's silence makes their history and culture like a black continent. However, she believes that as long as women can write, they will must create a new history and enhance a special culture. They have to be very careful during the process of writing. The narrow life experience limits their writing abilities, and most of them never travel. Therefore, the themes of their writings only focus on the domestic affairs. On the whole, what Woolf's feminism requires is not rights equality, but actually it is "humanitarianism" on higher significance. She exclaims that "the way of women liberation is so far that women should try to create a more suitable formality instead of out of date formality. It is after the completion of this mission that women can get freedom and achievement. Ability showed after the corrected position cannot be realized by this or that generation. Women energy has been sufficiently used and highly developed. However, the only way to combine surplus energy into the new formality is the same involvement and liberation of both man and woman."[14]

Last but not least, unlike previous feminism, Virginia Woolf believes that it is patriarchy that is the root of female lower social position and political rights. Patriarchal pattern means a society in which man is the center and woman is the oppressive. All authoritative position is set for male and male's criteria can be used to appraise female in the patriarchal society; on the other hand, patriarchy emphasizes that male temperament is normal and perfect, but female figure is subordinate and interior. Patriarchy considers that male is the center of the world, and all the rules are in men's hand and all the society should serve for man, while female are subordinate and must obey to male. Woolf does not believe in patriarchy's idea and, on the contrary, she believes that patriarchy constrains people's thoughts and lulls people's manners. She also believes that in patriarchal society, men can easily distort the truth, ignore the freedom of academic and culture. They are full of desires on money, right and control. These desires cause tyranny. Woolf experiencing the misery caused by the World War I, says that "War is a profession for man. It is the source of joy and excitement as well as the realization of male's character." By saying these sentences, Woolf reveals that men are not as noble and as perfect as the patriarchy describes. They are aggressive and women have their merits: they are peaceful.

In Woolf's eyes, the oppression of patriarchy lies in psychological, economic and social factors. The legitimate innovation for changing women's position is not enough. As time goes on, the system of patriarchal political, ideology and culture have been strengthened and consolidated. Owing to the deep influence of patriarchy, there is need for a rudimentary arduous revolution. Woolf's novels, especially *Mrs. Dalloway* and *To the Lighthouse*, are devoted to portray a picture of a patriarchal and imperialistic society, and to detail the factors that have limited women's opportunities for a meaningful life. In both novels, women suffer alone, have no chances for education, lack warmth and are compelled to suppress their needs. Virginia Woolf aimed at communicating the message that such a blind social system must be eradicated from its roots.

Notes

1. The Enlightenment is a European intellectual movement of the late 17th and 18th centuries emphasizing reason and individualism rather than tradition. It was heavily influenced by 17th century philosophers such as Descartes, Locke, Newton and so on.

2. The Chartism Movement was a UK parliament reform movement driven by the working classes. It grew following the failure of the *1832 Reform Act* to extend the vote beyond those owning property. It was drawn up for the London Working Men's Association (LWMA) by William Lovett and Francis Place with six demands:

All men should have the vote (universal manhood suffrage). Voting should take place by secret ballot. Parliamentary elections should take place every year, not once every five years. Constituencies should be of equal size. Members of Parliament should be paid. The property qualification for becoming a member of Parliament should be abolished.

3. The Civil Rights Movement (1954–1968) is a term that encompasses the strategies, groups, and social movements in the United States whose goals were to end racial segregation and discrimination against African Americans and to secure legal recognition and federal protection of the citizenship rights enumerated in the Constitution and federal law.

4. The Second Feminism Wave is a period of feminist activity and thought that first began in the early 1960s in the United States, and eventually spread throughout the Western world and beyond. In the United States the movement lasted through the early 1980s. It later became a worldwide movement that was strong in Europe and parts of Asia. Whereas first-wave feminism focused mainly on suffrage and overturning legal obstacles to gender equality (e. g. voting rights and property rights), second-wave feminism broadened the debate to a wide range of issues: sexuality, family, the workplace, reproductive rights, de facto inequalities, and

official legal inequalities. Second-wave feminism also drew attention to domestic violence and marital rape issues, establishment of rape crisis and battered women's shelters, and changes in custody and divorce law.

5. Elizabeth Cleghorn Gaskell, (née Stevenson; September 29, 1810–November 12, 1865), often referred to as Mrs Gaskell, was an English novelist and short story writer. Her novels offer a detailed portrait of the lives of many strata of Victorian society, including the very poor, and are of interest to social historians as well as lovers of literature. Her first novel, *Mary Barton*, was published in 1848. Gaskell's *The Life of Charlotte Brontë*, published in 1857, was the first biography of Brontë. Some of Gaskell's best known novels are *Cranford* (1851–1853), *North and South* (1854–55), and *Wives and Daughters* (1865).

6. *Jane Eyre* is the materpiece of Charlotte Brontë, a British novelist, which is considered the model of the independent woman in the world.

7. Alexandrina Victoria (May 24, 1819–January 22, 1901) was Queen of the United Kingdom of Great Britain and Ireland from June 20, 1837 until her death. From May 1, 1876, she adopted the additional title of Empress of India. Her reign of 63 years and 7 months is known as the Victorian era and was longer than that of any of her predecessors. It was a period of industrial, cultural, political, scientific, and military change within the United Kingdom, and was marked by a great expansion of the British Empire. She was the last British monarch of the House of Hanover. Her son and successor, Edward VII, inaugurated the House of Saxe-Coburg and Gotha.

8. *Mary Barton* is one of the works of Mrs Gaskell, *a Tale of Manchester Life* (published anonymously in 1848), an attack on the behavior of factory employers during the 1840s, a time of depression and hardship for the British working class. This paper won her the friendship of Charles Dickens, who requested a contribution to his new magazine, *Household Words*. Between 1851 and 1853 Gaskell contributed the papers later published under the title of *Cranford* (1853). This book, concerning elegant gentility among women in a country town, has become an English classic.

9. Stella is one of Woolf's sisters who is obident to her father like her mother, so she is seriously ill, and dies of Peritonitis at last.

10. Laura Stephen is Woolf's another sister who is different from Stella, a little rebellions to her father and refuses the control of the parents. She is considered to be evil and deserved harsh punishments. So she is restricted in an attic away from

others.

11. Barrett, Michele (ed). Virginia Woolf: Women and Writing [C]. New York and London: Harcouri Brace Jo-vanovich. 1980, p. 97.

12. Woolf, Virginia. Three Guineas [M]. London: Honarlh, 1968, p. 24.

13. 弗吉尼亚·伍尔夫:《伍尔夫随笔全集》,王义国等译,中国社会科学出版社,第1837页。

Chapter Four　Her Unique Skill of Stream of Consciousness

4.1　The Theory of Stream of Consciousness

According to the encyclopedia, stream of consciousness, in literature, relates to the technique that records the multifarious thoughts and feelings of a character without regard to logical argument or narrative sequence. The writer attempts by the stream of consciousness to reflect all the forces, external and internal, influencing the psychology of a character at a single moment. The origin of the stream of consciousness employed in literature, may be dated back to the long monologues in Shakespeare's dramas. It also has a very close relationship with the traditional psychological novels in the 18th century Lawrence Sterne, a famous novelist in the 18th century figured a child's inner world and psychological development in his work *Tristram Shandy*. Edouard Dufardin[1], a French novelist, used the technique of interior monologue in his novel *Les Lauriers Sont Coupes* (1887). It's regarded as the beginning of the stream of consciousness novel in modern literary creation.

The technique was first employed by Edouard Dujardin (1861–1949) in his novel *Les Lauriers* sont coupes (1888) and the phrase "stream of consciousness" to indicate the flow of inner experience was first used by William James in *Principles of Psychology*. (1890) Instead of agreeing with his contemporaries about consciousness being "chopped up in bits", William James took the innovative step towards describing the human mind as a "stream of thought or consciousness".

Soon after, this scientific theory was adapted into a literary term. M. Abrams asserts that a stream of consciousness narrative "describes the unbroken flow of perceptions, thoughts, and feelings in the waking mind." Many authors during this time period were influenced by the new psychological ideas that were becoming accepted as ways to identify the true reality of human consciousness. Psychologist Sigmund Freud[3] stepped onto this scene, too. His emphasis on individuals interconnection made up of the id, ego, and the super ego parallels well with how new authors began to characterize using not only spoken words, but also by writing streams of thought possibly going through the characters' minds.

As Robert Humphrey[4] states, "subject matter ... for the earlier novelists are motive and action (external man) and for the later ones, psychic existences and functioning (internal man)." Additionally Humphrey points out how this new narrative form "presents the character more accurately and more realistically". All narration and description should come out from the sense, observation and mind of this character. Although James is not a novelist of stream of consciousness, his opinion about the form and reality is obviously an influential factor of stream of consciousness novels.

Marcel Proust[5] also contributed a lot to the theory of stream of consciousness. The form of his novel is like an envelope, which is flexible and can contain various contents, including inner reality and outside world. The traditional form of novels has not satisfied the requirement of modern novels, because the former is unable to reflect the inner reality that modernist writers pursue. "Whether we call it life or spirit, truth or reality, this, the essential thing, has moved off, and refuses to be contained any longer in such ill-fitting vestments as we provide."

When the development of stream of consciousness theory is discussed, Henry James has to be mentioned. Henry James is an American novelist who is the first one to write psychological analysis novels. He pays much attention to reality. In his famous critical essay *The Art of Fiction* (1884), James expresses his opinion of novel in this way: "... I may therefore venture to say that the air of reality seems to me to be the supreme virtue of a novel ..." His concept of reality is "impression of life", which is what writers should reflect. James figures out that the consciousness of character is the core of works.

Therefore the task of modern novelists is to explore the suitable form because of "the infinite possibilities of the art". As what Woolf says, "Any method is right. Every method is right. That expresses what we wish to express, if we are writers; that brings us closer to the novelist's intention if we are readers."[6] In the 1920s, with the joint efforts of James Joyce and Virginia Woolf, the English "stream of consciousness" novel flourished. James Joyce's great work, *Ulysses*, is a masterpiece of stream-of-consciousness novels. His works influenced Woolf a lot. Virginia Woolf thought highly of this great master. In her late works, she wrote like Joyce. As she ever commented, in contrast with those whom they have called materialist, Mr. Joyce is spiritual; he is concerned at all costs to reveal the flickering of that innermost flame that flashes its messages through the brain. Virginia Woolf stressed that novelists should change their focal point from materialism to spiritualism. She believed that it was the nature of characters that novelists really need to express. What novelists should be caring about was the internal world not the external world around the character.

Virginia Woolf, throughout her whole artistic life, never stopped experimenting with an effective artistic form to pursue the "interior reality" in the field of prose fiction. To Woolf, reality is objective, yet people's responses to the same objective reality are different. Owing to the changes of the times and the circumstances and the difference instance and viewpoint, people's sense of reality differs greatly. Woolf's reality, obviously, refers to people's interior sense of the objective reality, a kind of interior reality obtained through distilling the objective reality in one's consciousness. Woolf never hesitates to seek the true meaning of reality. She holds that reality is made of various impressions accumulated in the depths of our consciousness and at the same time continuously surging to the surface of our consciousness.

In the view of Woolf, fiction should move away from the traditional way. She thinks that traditional novel is just recording dull uninteresting trivial and less important things. The characters in which seem flat, inflexible and lack of sense of reality. Therefore, she strongly revolted against the traditional stereotyped form of fiction, and meanwhile, she tries to seek a more delicate rendering of those aspects of consciousness in which she feels the truth of human experience really lies. In her *Modern Fiction*, she expresses her own ideas about what is appropriate for fiction :

Examine for a moment an ordinary mind on an ordinary day. The mind receives a myriad impressions ... trivial, fantastic, evanescent, or engraved with the sharpness of steel. From all sides they come, an incessant shower of innumerable atoms; and as they falls, as they shape themselves into the life of Monday or Tuesday, the accent falls differently from of old; the moment of importance came not here but there; so that, if a writer ... could write what he chose, ... there would be no plot, on

comedy, no tragedy, ...[7]

These words reflect Woolf's point of view of writing fiction. She appeals to writers to focus on the inner world of characters in a fiction and show life by the way people experience. In her opinion, "Life is not a series of gig-lamps symmetrically arranged, life is luminous halo, a semitransparent envelope surrounding us from the beginning of consciousness to the end." Therefore, it is "the task of the novelist to convey this varying, this unknown spirit, whatever aberration or complexity it may display, with as little mixture of the alien and external as possible."[8]

4.2 Virginia Woolf's Literary Techniques of Stream of Consciousness

Virginia Woolf, with her distinctive narrative style and penetrating insight into the human psyche, is generally regarded as one of the finest English writers. She is a productive and accomplished writer of novels, essays and biographies. In her literary practices, she had been contributing to the formation of modernism. Virginia Woolf has altogether written ten novels which can be roughly divided into two groups. One group is composed of her stream of consciousness novels and the other those written in the realist tradition. Five of her stream of consciousness novels and the short story, *The Mark on the Wall*, are chosen as objects for analysis. They are *Jacob's Room*, *Mrs. Dalloway*, *To the Lighthouse*, *The Waves* and *Between the Acts*.

4.2.1 Free Association

Free association is a technique used in psychoanalytic therapy to help patients learn more about what they are thinking and feeling. It is most commonly associated with Sigmund Freud, who was the founder of psychoanalytic therapy. Freud used free association to help his patients discover unconscious thoughts and feelings that had been repressed or ignored. When his patients became aware of these unconscious thoughts or feelings, they were better able to manage them or change problematic behaviors.

The goal of free association is not primarily to uncover hidden memories but to identify genuine thoughts and feelings about life situations that might be problematic, yet not be self-evident. For example, a woman might tell herself and others that she loves the people she works with but ends up avoiding her colleagues most of the time. Free association would be a helpful technique to explore the conflict or tension between these two competing attitudes.

Woolf employs free association in exploring character's inner world. *The Mark on the Wall* reveals a character's spiritual activities. It is a masterpiece of "free association". Throughout the short piece, the character is sitting in a chair. There is no movement, no plot, no tragedy, no comedy, no love interest, not to mention description of the exterior world except the object —the mark on the wall. Obviously, *The Mark on the Wall* is quite against the traditional way of novel writing. No matter in style or in artistic from, *The Mark on the Wall* is the breakthrough to the traditional writing of fiction. It lays a solid foundation for the novel of the stream of consciousness. Woolf succeeded in employing her own point of views about the stream of consciousness in her short works.

The mark on the wall becomes the media connecting the internal world and external one. The snail has hard outside shell and soft interior, which maybe respectively, symbolized to the solid reality the consciousness. Therefore, it is likely that the snail is a perfect symbol of the combination of the two. In it, the author retreats out of the fiction, and makes the readers directly face the character and even the inner conscious of the character of the work. The short story only focuses on some fragments of thoughts flashes through the brain and instant impression occurs in the mind, but it portrays and captures "the moment of importance".

In *The Mark on the Wall*, Woolf talks about the heroine's reveries when she notices a mark on the wall of her sitting room. About what the mark really is, her trains of thought jump from one thing to another. First of all, she thinks that the mark must have been made by a nail for a miniature of a lady, and imagines the lady's taste and the reason of her moving why her moving away. But then she suddenly doubts her speculation and thinks "if I got up and looked at it, ten to one I shouldn't be able to say for certain; because once a thing's done, one ever knows how it happened." At the moment, the heroine thinks of life the mark on the wall again, thinking it may be caused by some round black substance, such as a small rose leaf left over from the summer. Following that, a series of associations occur to her —Shakespeare, the reign of Charles the First, Sunday afternoon walks, etc. And "In certain lights that mark on the wall seems actually to project from the wall", which subsequently makes her think of tombs. However, not very long the heroine comes to be deeply sunk into another series of free imagination, and what is more, she even thinks of an antiquary, a retired colonel and foot of a Chinese murderess at the local museum, etc. Constantly stimulated by the particular external stimulus, the heroine opens up the world of speculation and wild imagination. And sometimes she even does so by daring to deny the importance of long established convention, such as, which archbishop is followed by which archbishop, therefore "let Nature comfort you". But, after all, the heroine feels she must learn what on earth the mark on the wall is, and then she begins to associate it with something definite and real, such as "a plank in the sea", which makes her have "a satisfying sense of reality". Obviously, it is a masterpiece of "free association", which is a striking feature of novel of the stream of consciousness.

The heroine's mediation and thoughts constantly move far away from the particle of so called solid reality —what the mark on the wall really is. For Woolf, what is outside—the mark on the wall —is nothing more than a trigger for the character's mediation and wild imaginations, which somewhat present the life of the heroine herself, moving freely through time and space until the surrounding "present moment" is virtually forgotten. In other words, the mark on the wall seems to become the center of the heroine's conscious activities as well as the only media of the association between interior world and exterior world.

In fact, the narration of *The Mark on the Wall* is a record of a thought process. Throughout the works the heroine is being indulged in thought, meditation and imagination: "I want to think quietly, calmly, spaciously, never to be interrupted, never to rise from my chair, to slip easily from one thing to another, without any sense of hostility, or obstacle. I want to sink deeper and deeper, away from the surface, with its hard separate facts." While thinking, she seems reluctant to get up and look at the mark more closely to arrive at an answer. She tells herself "if I were to get up at this very moment and ascertain that the mark on the wall is really —what shall we say? What should I gain?"

As soon as she describes the solid objects, she brings them sensuously to life. And once she has done that, she cannot help daydreaming. Obviously, she is at "the significant moment" of recollecting the past things and thinking of life at random. Seemingly, her imagination and conscious illogically and unreasonably connected, but all thoughts being full of fragments and flowing stream of thought revolve around the center —the mark on the wall. The character in the fiction attempts constantly to apply new images to the mark on the wall, and thinks accordingly. While doing so, she achieves a sense of being set free and self-enjoying at "the significant moment" and "feels a satisfying sense of reality". To her, that is "something definite, something real". Gradually her conscious becomes obscure and unclear. She can't remember a thing at all. "Everything's moving, falling, slipping, vanishing..." At this very moment, her thoughts are interrupted suddenly by a voice:

"I'm going out to buy a newspaper."

"Yes ?"

"Though it's no good buying newspapers ... Nothing ever happens. Curse this war; God damn this war! ... All the same, I don't see why we should have a snail on our wall." [9] As a result, the heroine is drawn back to the reality, and she finally comes to realize "the mark on the wall was a snail." With the moment of illumination, "the significant moment" comes to an end.

Seemingly, the work itself is concerned with what the mark really is, however, what is concerned with is the question of how important the world of fact is. In the course of the narration, the heroine is repeatedly drawn back to the reality, the mark on the wall. Probably, she is nearsighted, but she seems unwilling to rise to look at it closely to get an answer. When the truth about the mark become known at the end, the story stops as well. Then, the meditation of the character comes to an end, or more exactly speaking, her free association can even be considered to be destroyed by the factual information. Therefore, we can say the short novel of stream of consciousness presents a "moment of importance". Although the period of time in which the story takes place probably lasts at most no more than ten minutes, the narration covers a very rich spiritual world, including the past and the present, the history and the reality, life and death; various pictures and sights appear in the mind of the character, and flow like a stream. Woolf considers this moment her subject as well as the true reality, because it is at the very important moment that the character thinks about and pursues life and the world. To the heroine, life is full of mystery just like the mark on the wall. *The Mark on the Wall* demonstrates Woolf's point of view on the stream of consciousness successfully and lays a firm foundation for her later novel of stream of consciousness.

4.2.2 Interior Monologue

Interior monologue is a phrase closed related to the stream of consciousness novel. Unlike external action, the movement of consciousness is a psychological process which we can not see. So an objective description of it is impossible and interior monologue, which can register the slightest wavering of or the world that surrounds consciousness, is the best way to illustrate it. Almost all the stream of consciousness novelists use this technique in their works.

Stream of consciousness is a very complicated psychological process. According to the Austrian psychoanalyst Sigmund Freud, it can be divided into three levels: the Id (the unconscious), the Ego (the subconscious) and the Superego (the conscious). Of the three levels, the unconscious mind is the most primitive state of mind. To show the different levels of one's consciousness, interior monologue is also divided into different types. Generally speaking, interior monologue can be divided into two types: direct interior monologue and indirect interior monologue. When direct interior monologue is used, the author adopts the first person to narrate and is not involved in the narration by making no explanation or remark on the character's thought and experience. This device enables the character to thoroughly reveal his/her complex psychological activity and particularly it enables a display of the character's unconsciousness. The display of the unconscious part of the character gives the reader a chance to a fuller and deeper understanding of the character.

When indirect interior monologue is used, the author will use the third person to narrate and is partly involved in the narration by making some explanation or comment. This device enables the writer to show the workings of the conscious and subconscious mind but not that of the unconscious mind since the movement of the character's consciousness is controlled surreptitiously by the writer. Virginia Woolf and James Joyce are masters of the stream of consciousness novel and both adopt the technique of interior monologue. However, Woolf tends to use indirect interior monologue while Joyce usually uses direct interior monologue.

Examples of indirect interior monologue can be found in many parts of Mrs. Dalloway written by Woolf:

So she would still find herself arguing in St. James's Park, still making out that she had been right—and she had too—not to marry him. For in marriage a little license, a little independence there must be between people living together day in and day out in the same house, which Richard gave her, and him. (Where was he this morning for instance? Some committee, she never asked what.) But with Peter every thing had to be shared; everything gone into. And it was intolerable, and when it came that scene in the little garden by the fountain, she had to break with him or they would have been destroyed, both of them ruined, she was convinced; though she had borne about with her for years like an arrow sticking in her heart, the grief, the anguish; and then the horror of the moment when someone told her at the concert that he had married a woman met on the boat going to India! Never should she forget all that! Cold, heartless, a prude, he called her. Never could she understand how he cared. But those Indian women did presumably—silly, pretty, flimsy nincompoops. And she wasted her pity. For he was quite happy, he assured her—perfectly happy, though he had never done a thing that they talked of his whole life had been a failure. It made her angry still.[10]

Peter is Clarissa's former love. Compared with her husband, Peter is fantastic, a little bit dominant but not practical. Though she finally chooses Mr. Dalloway as her husband, she still loves Peter. That is why she feels horrible when she is informed of Peter's marriage with an Indian girl. Like any other sensitive woman, she becomes jealous of the Indian girl and calls her "silly, pretty, flimsy nincompoop". After many years of peaceful but dull marriage life with Mr. Dalloway, her mood is stirred by the news of Peter's returning to London from India. So she is trying to convince herself that her choice of Mr. Dalloway as her husband is right. This is a subtle description of the psychology of a sensitive woman. This is not a one-hundred-percent indirect interior monologue but more like a kind of internal analysis made by the writer. In this sense, Virginia Woolf is unique in using the technique of indirect interior monologue.

In most cases, Virginia Woolf uses indirect interior monologue. But it does not mean she never uses direct interior monologue. In some cases, she adopts direct interior monologue, too. The following is an example of her direct interior monologue:

Curse you then. However beat and done with it all I am, I must haul myself up, and find the particular coat that belongs to me; must push my arms into the sleeves; must muffle myself up against the night air and be off. I, tired as I am, spent as I am, and almost worn out with all this rubbing of my nose along the surfaces of things, even I, an elderly man who is getting rather heavy and dislikes exertion, must take myself of and catch some last train.[11]

This passage is from her novel *The Waves*. It is the direct interior monologue of Bernard, one of the six characters. Throughout his life, Bernard has been trying to find the meaning of life. But he fails to have an answer even when he comes to his old age. Though he is exhausted, he determines to have a last try. The direct interior monologue above reveals his determination. Comparing this direct interior monologue of Virginia Woolf with that of Joyce, we fail to find such situations as ellipsis of punctuations, dislocation of grammar and syntax, and broken words in Mrs. Woolf's direct interior monologue as we do in that of Joyce. In Mrs. Woolf's direct interior monologue, punctuations are there, grammar and syntax are correct, and there are no broken words.

Why does Virginia Woolf tend to use indirect interior monologue in her novels or why does she not go to the extreme as Joyce does by using ellipsis of punctuations, dislocation of grammar and syntax, and broken words even when she uses direct interior monologue? This is maybe because her acceptance of experiment does not extend to anarchy or to irresponsible eccentricity. It is true that Virginia Woolf is widely admired by her technical innovation in the novel and she expresses her readiness to welcome any experimental technique which achieves its effect.

4. 2. 3 Symbolic Imagery

As it is mentioned above, the stream of consciousness is a very complex psychological process and it can be divided into different levels. According to the Austrian psychoanalyst Sigmund Freud, it can be divided into three levels: the Id (the unconscious), the Ego (the subconscious) and the Superego (the conscious). The conscious mind can be described directly in demonstrative, ideographic and logical speech. But the subconscious mind, particularly the unconscious mind is usually a kind of sensual impression or reverie which is so complex, so elusive and so subtle that it is indescribable. When the demonstrative, ideographic and logical speech is not functional to describe the subconscious mind, particularly the unconscious mind, the stream of consciousness novelists, the main purpose of whom is to present to the reader the subconscious particularly unconscious mind of characters, have to find a special vehicle to do it. The special vehicle they find is symbolic imagery. This is because the unconscious mind, the most primitive state of one's mind, forms in the same way a symbol forms. To metaphysically present the sensual impressions and the hazy mood, which perch at the recesses of one's consciousness like the unconscious mind, the stream of consciousness novelists have to use symbolic imagery. As a novelist of this genre, Virginia Woolf is not an exception. So symbolic images can be found in each of her stream of consciousness novels.

In *Jacob's Room*, a symbolic image is the image of Jacob's room:

Lifeless is the air in an empty room, just swelling the curtain; the flowers in the jar shift. One fiber in the wicker arm-chair creaks, though no one sits there.[12]

This is a description of Jacob's room after his death in the war. His room becomes empty and lifeless. Even the air in the room seems not moving. Does it really become empty? In fact, there is not much change in the room as his friend Bonamy marvels when he enters Jacob's room "He left everything just as it was". His letters are there and his old shoes are there. Hadn't Jacob died in the war, his mother wouldn't have the feeling of emptiness. So this image of Jacob's room, which symbolizes Jacob's disappearance forever, is impressionistic. The impression of the room his mother gets when she enters the room is its emptiness. And this impression of her is closely related to her personal subjective mood—sadness caused by personal bereavement.

In *Mrs. Dalloway*, the clocks of London chime right through the book from start to finish. The clocks and the striking of the sound form a recurrent symbolic image. This is a quite complex image. The clocks and the striking of the sound are personified and endowed with the emotion of characters. Thus, this image symbolizes different things to different characters and it may mean different things even to the same character when the character is in different moods of him/her. When she crosses Victoria Street thinking of the quick passage of time, Clarissa Dalloway feels a suspense in her heart when she hears the striking of Big Ben. In this sense, the striking of the clock like a warning of the irrevocable hour symbolizes death. But on another occasion, the striking of the St. Margaret's clock makes her think of all sorts of little things such as Mrs. Marsham, Ellie Henderson and glasses for ices and have the feeling that "all sorts of little things came flooding and lapping and dancing in on the wake of that solemn stroke which lay flat like a bar of gold on the sea". In this sense, to Clarissa, the image of the clock and its striking becomes a symbol of life which is composed of countless little things. However, this image means different things for Peter Walsh. When he hears the striking of St. Margaret's clock in Clarissa's drawing room, Peter feels the sound of the clock is "like something alive". In Peter's imagination, Clarissa glides downstairs in white as the sound of the clock floats into the drawing room. But when he hears the sound of the high bell of the ambulance which carries Septimus's dead body, the striking of Big Ben becomes the tolling of the knell.

In *To the Lighthouse*, Virginia Woolf adopts the technique of symbolic imagery, too. The following is an example:

Mrs. Ramsay, who had been sitting loosely, folding her son in her arm, brace herself, and, half turning, seemed to raise herself with an effort, and at once to pour erect into the air a rain of energy, a column of spray, looking at the same time animated and alive as if all her energies were being fused into force, burning and illuminating (quietly though she sat, taking up her stocking again), and into this delicious fecundity, this fountain and spray of life, the fatal sterility of the male plunged itself, like a beak of brass, barren and bare. He said he wanted sympathy and he was a failure. Mrs. Ramsay flashed her needles. Mr. Ramsay repeated, never taking his eyes from her face, that he was a failure. She blew the words back at him. "Charles Tansley...," she said. But he must have more than that. It was sympathy he wanted, to be assured of his genius, first of all, and then to be taken within the circle of life, warmed and smoothed, to have his senses restored to him, his barrenness made fertile, and all the rooms of the house made full of life—the drawing room; behind the drawing room the kitchen; above the kitchen the bedrooms; and beyond them the nurseries; they must be furnished; they must be filled with life. [13]

This passage is an internal analysis of the consciousness of James, the youngest son of Mrs. Ramsay. In James's imagination, the image of his mother is a column of spray while the image of his father is a bird that sucks the column of spray greedily. Obviously the symbolic imagery here is impressionistic and it is a twisted personal impression which shows James's feeling but not others'. Compared with the symbolic imagery which means the same to all the characters, the personalized symbolic imagery may mean more and it can be used to express the character's subjective feeling and mood about something more complicated. James compares his mother to sweet spring water which can nourish all living things because his mother is a person of wide sympathies while he compares his father to a greedy bird that sucks the sweet spring water because his father is such a person who has no sympathy for others but always seeks sympathy from others. Since the symbolic image of his mother and that of his father are highly impersonalized and they show James' subjective feeling and mood, the connotation of the two images here is broadened. Thus, when we read the two symbolic images with our imagination, we can not only know James' impression of his parents but also sense his complicated mood of Oedipus complex.

The Waves is said to be a novel closest to poetry. So it is not surprising to find this novel is permeated with symbolic images which are rich in poetry. Among the many symbolic images, the image of waves is a major one. The waves gather forces and shapes at first, rise to a crest, then break up, and finally dissolve in a thin spread of foam. On the daytime, the waves sparkle and blaze gold under the sunshine. But they lose their gorgeousness when the sun sinks. Dusky sea and darkened sky become indistinguishable, and decayed leaves and frail cargo float on the oozy surface of the sea. This is the image of waves. The form of waves symbolizes the form of human life which is composed of birth, childhood, adolescence, youth, adulthood, old age and death. The wave is a part of nature. So the life-and-death cycle is a part of nature, too. Thus, the wave becomes a symbol of the eternality of the life-and-death cycle. Compared with the symbolic images in other novels of Virginia Woolf, the image of waves in this novel is served successfully to give the reader more poetic sense.

4.2.4 Multiple Inner Points of View

In the novels, the reader has to enter the characters' subjective worlds, in other words, the psychological depths of each of them. As the stories develop, as every character is related with each other, the reader is presented with a spiritual world, very shifting and complex, with streams of memories, fantasies, fears, excitements and forebodings, with fluctuating moods and changeable feelings. The reader's attention is then drawn to these movements of consciousness, or the free penetration of character's consciousness. Confronted with this jumble of thoughts, he is forced to construct an evaluation of the novel for himself based on his own value system. The narrative technique of this kind focuses on the very mental process of the character and digs out every piece of human psyche, as is tenured the "multiple inner points of view" narration.

In most traditional novels, the writers must decide who will relate the stories to the readers and the choices open to them are numerous. The one who serves this function is known as the narrator. The readers, therefore, perceive the story of a novel to a greater or lesser extent through the narrator's point of view. It is obvious, therefore, that the narrator becomes extremely important in guiding the readers' judgments through a novel, and it is through the narrator's language that events and characters are depicted. There are usually two types of narrators in most novels. The first is known as omniscient narrator—the story is told by an omniscient narrator, who has access to all the events as well as to the thoughts of his characters. An omniscient narrator can make free comments on anything he wants. Through his emphasis of certain characters and events, through his manipulation of imagination and language, this omniscient narrator, either conspicuously or not, serves as an interpreter or a bridge between the reader and the events in a novel; the second type is the first person or the third person narrator. By choosing this narrative perspective, the narrator is restricting himself to a single character's perspective. Such narration will be limited by that character's intelligence and by his moral and social values. The narrator—agent for this type of narration could be either the first person (I) or the third person (he, she, it, they).

In Woolf's narrative strategy—the multiple inner points of view narration, she deliberately provides the reader with more than one narrative perspective instead of restricting the narration to single narrative point of view. In other words, the novels have several kinds of narrators who lead different narrative strands; they can penetrate different characters' consciousnesses and juggles with them. In *To the Lighthouse*, according to Leaska, "Almost half the first section is transmitted through Mrs. Ramsay; more than three quarters of the second section is given omnisciently; and more than half of the third section is filtered through Lily Briscoe." So the reader encounters not only the omniscient narrator but also the third person or even the first person narrator. Besides, this narrative method puts the emphasis on how the character experiences rather than what is experienced, so what matters in the novel is the moment's thinking and feeling as they are remembered by each other. With these jumble of thoughts from different points of view, the reader's sense of the novel becomes very shifting and unstable; he can barely find any single, privileged, objective and external point of view, on which the whole truth can depend; as he listens to them all, he has to make up his mind like a jury for himself. So, the narrative is based on several different perspectives by different narrators interwoven together, first person, third person or omniscient. The following passages will stand as illustrations for this narrative technique based on the two novels.

At the beginning of *Mrs. Dalloway*, a mystery arises from an expensive car breaking down with an explosion outside the florist's shop where Mrs. Dalloway is buying flowers for her party. An unknown narrator describes the situation on the street:

Yet rumors were at once in circulation from the middle of Bond Street to Oxford Street on one side, to Atkinson 's scent shop on the other . . . But nobody knew whose face had been seen. Was it the Prince of Wales's, the Queen's, the Prime Minister's? Whose face was it? Nobody knew. Every one looked at the motor car. Septimus looked. Boys on bicycles sprang off. Traffic accumulated. And there the motor car stood, with drawn blinds, and upon them a curious pattern like a tree.[14]

Here, several conscious strands are speculating about who is in the car. Mrs. Dalloway's first thought was that "Oh! A pistol shot in the street outside!" Then, when she comes out of the flower shop, she thinks it is the Queen in the car:

It is probably the Queen, thought Mrs. Dalloway coming out of Mulberry's with her flowers; the Queen. And for a second she wore a look of extreme dignity . . .[15]

Then the narrator moves the narrative strand to the insane shell-shock sufferer Septimus Warren Smith and his wife Lucrezia who are also thinking about the explosion. Septimus is in a panic, thinking that the commotion in the street must be his fault:

Septimus thought, and this gradual drawing together of everything to one center before his eyes, as if some horror had come almost to the surface and was about to burst into flames, terrified him. The world wavered and quivered and threatened to burst into flames. It is I who am blocking the way, he thought. Was he not being looked at and pointed at; was he not weighted there, rooted to the pavement, for a purpose? But for what purpose?[16] As the car moves away, as it goes towards Buckingham Palace, the omniscient narrator appears who recounts the crowd's patriotic reactions to it with an ironical tone:

At once they stood even straighter, and removed their hands, and seemed ready attend their Sovereign, if need be, to the cannon's mouth, as their ancestors had done before them. Shawled Moll Pratt with her flowers on the pavement wished the dear boy well (it was the Prince of Wales for certain) and would have tossed the price of a pot of beer—a bunch of roses—into St. James's Street out of sheer light heartedness and contempt of poverty had she not seen the constable's eye upon her, discouraging and old Irish woman's loyalty. Little Mr. Browley, . . . was sealed with wax over the deeper sources of life but could be unsealed suddenly, inappropriately, sentimentally by this sort of thing poor women waiting to see the Queen go past poor women, nice little children, orphans, widows, the War—, tut-tut—actually had tears in his eyes.[17]

Here, the narrative strands are shifting continuously among various narrators. They not only move smoothly from one character to another but also from the third person narrator to the omniscient narrator, or vice versa. At the end of this street scene narration, the trivial question about who is in the car remains unresolved. There is no objective voice, no omniscient narrator (obvious or otherwise), would serve as an interpreter between the reader and the events in the street and clarify for the reader this puzzle. The reader may discover that these speculations on who is in the car are rather everyday banalities, but the significance lies in that it faithfully records everybody's concerns at the moment, and these experiences of the moment is what Virginia Woolf is most concerned about. In fact, this street scene performs a narrative function of juxtaposing the main characters, Clarissa Dalloway, Septimus Smith, and later, Peter's consciousnesses together. Since the narrators enter the consciousnesses of these characters and expose them to the reader, the reader can thus form his first-step impressions on them from these initial contacts with the characters' mind and evaluates them according to his norms—his own value systems. Then, he may venture a guess that Mrs. Dalloway is a noble lady of dignity and Septimus seems to have the insane habit of delusion. As he reads further into the story, he comes to know that Mrs. Dalloway and Peter Walsh are two parallel narrative strands. Both are seeking the truth of the life, one is from the sane part; the other is from the insane part.

4.2.5 Shuffle of Time and Space

"Stream of consciousness" is originally a term in psychology. As a psychological term, it first appeared in a paper written by William James, an American psychologist, in 1884. Four years later, he had his book *The Principles of Psychology* published, in which he elaborated this term as follows:

Consciousness, then, does not appear to itself chopped up in bits. Such words as chain or train do not describe it fitly as it presents itself in the first instance. It is nothing jointed; it flows. A river or a stream are the metaphors by which it is most naturally described. In talking of it hereafter, let us call it the stream of thought, of consciousness, or of subjective life.[18] The phrase coined by Henry James gives us a vivid description of the flow of thoughts. Consciousness, waking as being of the mind and it suggests such characteristics of the movement of continuous and being ever-shifting. The shift may take place between the objective reality and the subjective reality, between different time or space. According to Henri Bergson, French philosopher, there are two kinds of time: physical time and psychological time. The two kinds of time do not go in the same direction. The physical time is measured by second, minute and hour while the psychological time has something to do with one's stream of consciousness which may flow from the present to the past in reminiscence or to the future in imagination. In the process of the movement of consciousness, which follows the psychological time, the past, present and future are shuffled and overlapped, and different scenes in space may swarm into one's mind in a twinkling or the same scene in space may appear in the mind of different people, leaving them different impressions.

In short, the frequent shift in time and space is one pattern of the flow of consciousness. To show the shift in time and space when the stream of consciousness of their characters is portrayed, stream of consciousness novelists invent the technique of shuffle of time and space. When this technique is used, most novelists will use the device of montage which is basically a device used in film. Montage can be divided into two types: time montage and space montage. When time montage is used, the stream of consciousness of characters flows from the present to past or to future against the same frame of place setting.

An example of time montage can be found in the first part of *Mrs. Dalloway*:

Mrs. Dalloway said she would buy the flowers herself. For Lucy had her work cut out for her. The doors would be taken off their hinges; Rumpel mayer's men were coming. And then, thought Clarissa Dalloway, what a morning—fresh as if issued to children on a beach. What a lark! What a plunge! For so it had always seemed to her when, with a little squeak of the hinges, which she could hear now, she had burst open the French windows and plunged at Bourton into the open air. How fresh, how calm, stiller than this. Of course, the air was in the early morning; like the flap of a wave the kiss of a wave; chill and sharp and yet (for a girl of eighteen as she then was) solemn, feeling as she did, standing there at the open window, that something awful was about to happen; looking at the flowers, at the trees with the smoke winding off them and the rocks rising, falling; standing and looking until Peter Walsh said, "Musing among the vegetables? I prefer men to cauliflowers." Was that it? He must have said it at breakfast one morning when she had gone out on to the terrace—Peter Walsh. He would be back from India one of these days, June or July, she forgot which, for his letters were awfully dull; it was his sayings one remembered; his eyes, his pocket-knife, his smile, his grumpiness and, when millions of things had utterly vanished—how strange it was—a few sayings like this about cabbages. She stiffened a little on the kerb, waiting for Durtnall's van to pass. A charming woman, Scrope Purvis thought her (knowing her as one does know people who live next door to one in Westminster); a touch of the bird about her, of the jay, blue-green, light, vivacious, though she was over fifty, and grown very white since her illness. There she perched, never seeing him, waiting to cross, very upright. For having lived in Westminster—how many years now? Over twenty. One feels even in the midst of the traffic, or waking at night. Clarissa was positive, a particular hush, or solemnity; an indescribable pause; a suspense ...[19]

This passage is from the very beginning of the novel, which starts with Clarissa Dalloway's thinking of buying flowers for her party which will be held in the evening. Then her train of thought comes back to the present when she opens the door. The fresh air in the morning outside the door triggers her free association and her stream of consciousness flows to the physical time of twenty years ago when she is only eighteen years old living in Bourton where she fells in love with Peter Walsh, a conversation with whom is deeply rooted in her memory. After that, her stream of consciousness flows to the future again when she thinks of the news that Peter is coming back to London from India. When she is waiting to cross the street, her beauty arouses her neighbour Scrope Purvis's comment on her. The omniscient narration of what Purvis thinks about her indicates the present. Then her indirect interior monologue about her special feeling towards Westminster in which she is living now shows that her stream of consciousness flows back from the future to the present. In spite of the frequent shift in time, the narration is smooth due to the fact that the psychological time sequence is continued when the physical time sequence is disrupted. In this example, besides the shift in time, there is the shift between the mind of Purvis and that of Clarissa. To mark the shift between the mind of one character and that of another, Virginia Woolf uses some special words as signposts. The word "for" which is often used to commence a paragraph is such a signpost. To Virginia Woolf, this word is her conjunction, whose purpose is to indicate the vague, pseudo-logical connection between the different sections of a reverie. The word "one" is another signpost. To Virginia Woolf, this word is an indeterminate kind of pronoun between the third personal pronoun and the first personal pronoun. With these two signposts, Virginia Woolf succeeds in guiding the reader to shift from the mind of one character to that of another without the narration giving the reader sense of being disrupted.

4.2.6 The Free Indirect Speech

After we have discussed Virginia Woolf's use of multiple inner points of view narration: the events and characters are perceived and interpreted through a variety of narrative perspectives so as to produce a distinct effect that forces the reader to make his own judgment. However, as we probe deep into this narrative technique, especially as we look into every special narrative strand, we feel compelled to tackle this problem—how are the multiple inner points of view presented? Or, how does the narrator present the stream of consciousness to the reader? As a stream-of-consciousness writer, Woolf, as others do, focuses her novels entirely on the mental process of her characters. However, these stream-of-consciousness writers differ greatly in that they have their own ways of presenting the consciousness.

In the case of Woolf, she often represents the consciousness indirectly. In other words, she edits and recounts the conscious streams instead of directly presenting the fragments of words or sentences similar to human thoughts as James Joyce does in Finnegans Wake or Ulysses. Woolf's narrative method of this kind has two distinct features: first, it represents the thoughts in indirect speech and not always indicates the sources; it also clings closely enough to the tenors of consciousnesses and imitating their verbal style, which gives the sense more of direct speech than indirect speech; second, it keeps very close to the characters' conscious streams and put into words their subtle experiences or beautiful images, for which the characters remain inarticulate. These verbalized experiences or images may be incipiently fragmentary in the characters' minds, but the narrator poetically renders them. Therefore, this narrative method is generally referred to as the "free indirect speech".

In order to cast some light on this narrative strategy, let's first turn to the speeches in the traditional novels. In most nineteenth-century novels, the authors represent the characters' thoughts and saying mostly through two kinds of speeches: direct speech and indirect speech. In direct speech, a narrator directly quotes the words of a character, and this is usually signaled by the use of quotation marks; the other is indirect speech, in which the narrator reports to us what a character has said or thought by changing the tense or pronoun of it. These two kinds of speeches are

often seen in most traditional novel. In the early twentieth century, most novelists of modern fictions turned to the exploration of the inner worlds, rather than the concerns of external reality. Some novelists emphasize the prespeech levels of consciousness in order to reveal the psychic being of the character. Others recount the character's thoughts without a break in the narrative treads.

Therefore, the speech presentations or thought presentations come to be further diversified to meet the needs of literary creation. Genette proposes to divide the speeches into four categories: discours narrativise, discours transpose, discours rapporte, discours immdiat. G. N. Leech and M. H. Snort in the book of style in Fiction, put forwards five kinds of speech presentations: direct speech (DS), indirect speech (IS), free direct speech (FDS), free indirect speech (FIS), and narrative report of speech acts (NRSA). The latter classification by Leech and Snort is generally viewed as more acceptable. Chen Kai, in his paper *Language Styles in Mrs. Dalloway*, points out that DS is the conventional way of speech representing the "Norm" and these five kinds of speeches: NRSA, IS, FIS, DS and FDS are this arrayed according to the degree of the characters' freedom (contrasted by the degree of the author's intervention in the novel); He also points out that in *To the Lighthouse*, when Mrs. Ramsay volunteers to buy something for Mr. Carmichael on her way to the town, she is turned down unexpectedly. Then her sympathy for him immediately turns to bitterness and animosity. The narrative clings closely to the changes of Mrs. Ramsay's emotion, mimicking her angry words with free indirect speech:

But no, he wanted nothing. She told the story; an air at Oxford with some girl; an early marriage; poverty; going to India; translating a little poetry very beautifully, I believe being willing to teach the boys Persian or Hindustanee, but what really was the use of that? —and then lying, as they saw him, on the lawn.[20]

Here, when Mrs. Ramsay is turned down, her emotion is shifted from surprise to anger, and finally to the belittlement of Mr. Carmichael so as to seek a balance of mind. The narration of the above passage is fully in Mrs. Ramsay's perspective; it is presented in the form of indirect speech, but when the reader reads that, "What really was the use of that? —and then lying, as they saw him on the lawn", he seems to listen to the words actually spoken by Mrs. Ramsay due to a strong sense of mockery leaps from the text. The narrator sneaks into Mrs. Ramsay's consciousness and mimics her thought.

The free indirect speech as a narrative choice has its advantage to hold the tenor of a character's consciousness by ways of mimicking the verbal style as is in direct speech. It also allows the narrator to assemble, to put into words or images the character's moments of beings (stream of thoughts), which for the character remains nonverbal or which could not be fully spelled out in words. For example, in *To the Lighthouse*, near the end of the dinner party, Lily contemplates Mrs. Ramsay's sudden departure from dinner party and notices that dinner party disintegrates without her. Walking towards the nursery, Mrs. Ramsay reflects upon the moment of complete happiness she had felt during dinner party and her awareness of having accomplished something important in bringing together the different people who were present:

Not that she did in fact run or hurry; she went indeed rather slowly. She felt rather inclined just or a moment to stand still after all that chatter, and pick out one particular thing; the thing that mattered; ... It was windy. The stars themselves seemed to be shaking and darting light and trying to flash out between the edges of the leaves. Yes, that was done then, accomplished, and as with all things done, become solemn. Now one thought have been, only was shown now, and so being shown struck everything into stability. They would, she thought, going on again, however long they lived, come back to this night, this moon, this wind, this house, and to her. It flattered her, where she was most susceptible of flattery, to think how, wound about in their hearts, however long they lived she would be woven; and this, and this, and this, she thought ...[21]

The narrative point of the above passage is from Mrs. Ramsay. Although the narrator keeps very close to Clarissa's thoughts, the reader is not sure that she would genuinely speaks to herself inwardly the way as it is presented here. The narrator, using indirect speech, spells out her thoughts, ideas and images, which for her could be non-verbal or fragmented. Mrs. Ramsay knows she has created a memory, which will draw her guests together in time to come. She feels satisfied with her accomplishments. The narrator puts into images of what Mrs. Ramsay sees: "The stars themselves seemed to be shaking and darting light and trying to flash out between the edges of the leaves." Here these delighting images, which are so poetically rendered, are just flashing through Mrs. Ramsay's mind at the moment; the narrator catches them instantly and artfully recites them to convey her secret happiness of fulfillment in the dinner party: "Yes, that was done then, accomplished;

and as with all things done, become solemn." Mrs. Ramsay has once more proved her feminine desire to comfort every guest. However, using free indirect speech could only be effective when the above effects are desired. Despite its advantages, it poses some problems for the reader. In many of Woolf's novels, the narrative points of view shift constantly among different characters. Due to the use of free indirect speech, these consciousnesses often blend into each other without obvious indicators. Therefore, the reader may have difficulty in distinguishing the individual point of view. He has to make his own judgment from the content of the speech, or from the habitual usage of the character.

In *To the Lighthouse*, Mrs. Ramsay sits with her young son James when the family is talking about the next day's trip to the lighthouse. Despite Mrs. Ramsay's attempts to placate James, Mr. Ramsay continues to insist that the forthcoming visit to the lighthouse must be postponed. Young James is angered and hates his father very much:

Had there been and axe handy, a poker, or any weapon that would have gashed a hole in his father's breast and killed him, there and then, James would have seized it. Such were the extremes of emotion that Mr. Ramsay excited in his children's breast by his mere presence; (Omniscient narrator) standing, as now, lean as a knife, narrows the blade of one, grinning sarcastically, not only with the pleasure of disillusioning his son and casting ridicule upon his wife, who was ten thousand times better in every way than he was, (James's thought) but also with so secret conceit at his own accuracy judgment. What he said was true. It was always true. He was incapable of untruth; never tampered with a fact; never alter a disagreeable word to suit the pleasure or convenience of any mortal being, least of all of his own children, who, sprung from his loins, should be aware from childhood that life is difficult; facts uncompromising; and the passage to that fabled land where our brightest hopes are extinguished, our frail barks founder in darkness (her Mr. Ramsay would straighten his eyes upon the horizon), one that needs, above all, courage, truth, and the power to endure. (Mr. Ramsay's thought)[22]

In the above passage, because of the use of free indirect speech, the inexperienced reader may think that there is only one narrative voice here. But actually, there are three narrative voices working here, such as the omniscient narrator, young James and Mr. Ramsay. The omniscient narrator in the beginning sentences serves as a "stage direction" leading us to this particular setting—the conflicts between the father and the son. He generalizes the tenor of the whole passage, hostility and confrontation, "Such were the extremes of emotion that Mr. Ramsay excited in his children's breasts by his mere presence"; then, the narrative voice shifts subtly to James's point of view "not only with the pleasure of disillusioning his son and casting ridicule upon his wife, who was ten thousand times better in every way than he was". In this sentence, the reader can read between the lines that the son James is making a comparison between the parents, for he hates his father and thinks that his mother is far better than his father. Then the narrator stealthily takes Mr. Ramsay's point of view, "... one that needs, above all, courage, truth, and the power to endure." When the reader reads here, he is once more convinced that Mr. Ramsay is over-factual. There are several ways to distinguish these narrative strands in the free indirect speech.

One way of doing so is to grasp the content of each character's thought, the emotion it reveals, and the language it uses. The extreme hostility towards his father and Mr. Ramsay's excessive fondness of truth can indicate the sources of the narrative strands, which are sometimes contradictorily juxtaposed. Obviously, by identifying the attributions in the passages, such as he said, she thought, the reader can also distinguish the narrative voices. For example: She (Lily) felt curiously divided, as if one part of her were drawn out there—it was a still day, hazy.

This sentence is undoubtedly from Lily's. Therefore, the use of free indirect speech in Woolf's novels suggests that we have encountered a distinct technique that edits and recounts the character's inner point of view, which becomes the metaphor of stream of consciousness. It is obvious that the words on the pages (the free indirect speech), are not word-for-word transcription of the character's own interior monologue. She did not write down the interior monologue of the character, like that of Molly Bloom or Leopold Bloom, which are both full of incomplete sentences, disconcerting fragments, pieces of thought and perception that are most similar to the nature of human mentality. What she did instead is to provide new versions of the character's thoughts while maintaining the verbal style of them. There are several quite different techniques which are used to present stream-of-consciousness. So we can see *Mrs. Dalloway* and *To the Lighthouse* are mainly presented in narrated monologue in the form of free indirect speech.

Notes

1. Edouard Dufardin is a French novelist, the beginning of the stream of consciousness novel in modern literary creation, who had a great influnce on James Joyce's works.

2. Meyer Howard "Mike" Abrams (July 23, 1912-April 21, 2015), usually cited as M. H. Abrams, was an American literary critic, known for works on romanticism, in particular his book *The Mirror and the Lamp*. Under Abrams's editorship, *The Norton Anthology of English Literature* became the standard text for undergraduate survey courses across the U. S. and a major trendsetter in literary canon formation.

3. Sigmund Freud (May 6, 1856 - September 23, 1939, London, England), Austrian neurologist, founder of psychoanalysis. Freud may justly be called the most influential intellectual legislator of his age. His creation of psychoanalysis was at once a theory of the human psyche, a therapy for the relief of its ills, and an optic for the interpretation of culture and society. Despite repeated criticisms, attempted refutations, and qualifications of Freud's work, its spell remained powerful well after his death and in fields far removed from psychology as it is narrowly defined.

4. Robert L. Humphrey was an Iwo Jima veteran, Harvard graduate, and cross cultural conflict resolution specialist during the Cold War. He proposed the "Dual Life Value Theory" of Human Nature. Robert Humphrey defined the stream-of-consciousness fiction as "a type offiction in which the basic emphasis is placed on exploration of the prespeech levels of consciousness for the purpose, primarily, of revealing the psychic being of characters". Until Communism's fall, Humphrey kept his new methods confidential. Those methods are significant: (1) From his experiences with young infantrymen in heavy combat, and with the peasants in many villages of the world, he perceived humankind's basic goodness that philosophers have missed or under rated. (2) In place of compartmentalized, primarily mental

education, Humphrey has developed a human-nature-guided (moral, physical, artistic, mental) approach. He has since written *Values For A New Millennium and the Warrior Creed.*

5. Valentin Louis Georges Eugène Marcel Proust (July 10, 1871-November 18, 1922), known as Marcel Proust, was a French novelist, critic, and essayist best known for his monumental novel *À la recherche du temps perdu* (*In Search of Lost Time*, earlier rendered as *Remembrance of Things Past*), published in seven parts between 1913 and 1927. He is considered by critics and writers to be one of the most influential authors of the 20th century.

6. Virginia Woolf, Modern Fiction, from https://ebooks.adelaide.edu.au/w/woolf/virginia/w91c/chapter13.html.

7. Virginia Woolf, The Reader, New York and London: Harcourt Brace Jovanovich.

8. Virginia Woolf, The Reader, New York and London: Harcourt Brace Jovanovich.

9. Virginia Woolf, The Mark on the Wall, refers to http://www.bartleby.com/85/8.html.

10. Mrs. Dalloway: 10.

11. Virginia Woolf, The Waves, refers to http://www.feedbooks.com.

12. Jacob's Room, refers to http://www.feedbooks.com.

13. To the Lighthouse: 56-58.

14. To the Lighthouse. Foreword by Eudora Welty. San Diego: Harvestl Harcourt Brace Jovanovich, 1989 (1920). 19-20.

15. Mrs. Dalloway. San Diego: Harvest/Harcourt Brace Jovanovich, 1953 (1925): 23.

16. Mrs. Dalloway: 21.

17. Mrs. Dalloway: 26-28.

18. James, William. The Principles of Psychology. U.S.A.: The President and Fellows of Harvard College, 1983. 233.

19. Mrs. Dalloway. San Diego: Harvest/Harcourt Brace Jovanovich, 1953 (1925): 2-4.

20. To the Lighthouse: 14-15.

21. To the Lighthouse: 104-105.

22. To the Lighthouse: 9-10.

Chapter Five The Appreciation of Her Major Works

Virginia Woolf is one of the most prominent literary figures of the twentieth century. She is a versatile writer. Throughout her life she wrote book reviews, biographical and autobiographical sketches, social and literary criticism, personal essays, commemorative articles treating a wide range of topics, short stories and novels. Her short story collections: *Monday or Tuesday* (1921), *A Haunted House and Other Short Stories* (1944), *Mrs Dalloway's Party* (1973), *The Complete Shorter Fiction* (1985); Virginia Woolf published three books to which she gave the subtitle "A Biography": *Orlando*: *A Biography* (1928, usually characterized Novel, inspired by the life of Vita Sackville-West); *Flush*: *A Biography* (1933, more explicitly cross-genre: fiction as "stream of consciousness" tale by Flush, a dog; non-fiction in the sense of telling the story of the owner of the dog, Elizabeth Barrett Browning); *Roger Fry*: *A Biography* (1940); Non-fiction books or essay: other essays were collected in three volumes called *The Common Reader* (1925), *A Room of One's Own* (1929) and *The Common Reader*: *Second Series* (1932). After her death, her husband published a number of others, including *Three Guineas* (1938), *The Death of the Moth and Other Essays* (1942), *The Moment and Other Essays* (1947), *The Captain's Death Bed* (1950), *Hours in a Library* (1957), and *Granite and Rainbow* (1958), *Women and Writing* (1979) as well as a four-volume edition, *Collected Essays* (1966–1967). Besides these, Woolf's five diaries and four volumes of letters also belong to her essay works. *Drama Freshwater*: *A Comedy* (performed in 1923, revised in 1935, and published in 1976). Autobiographical writings and diaries: *A Writer's Diary* (1953) —Extracts from the complete diary, *Moments of Being* (1976), *A Moment's Liberty*: the shorter diary (1990), *The Diary of Virginia Woolf* (five volumes) —*Diary of Virginia Woolf* from 1915 to 1941, *Passionate Apprentice*: *The Early Journals*, 1897–1909 (1990), *Travels With*

Virginia Woolf (1993) —Greek travel diary of Virginia Woolf, edited by Jan Morris.

However, it has often been remembered of her that she is a novelist rather than an essayist, a critic, biographer, diarist or short story writer. Now, as we read her novels, especially her stream of consciousness novels, this judgment is firmly supported. There is no question that Virginia Woolf is at her best when she is writing her stream of consciousness novels which deal with the conscious, subconscious and even unconscious part of her. At the same time, Virginia Woolf is one of the most prominent writers in English literature feminist and she contributes a lot to feminism. Her life style and works embody her feminism attitudes. She portrayed the impact of the patriarchal English society on women's lives, the loneliness and frustration of women's lives that had been shaped by the moral, ideological and conventional factors. Many of her works reflected her philosophy of life and identification of women. Her novels held the key to the meaning of life and the position of women in the existing patriarchal society.

Virginia Woolf's career of fiction can be divided into three periods. At the first stage, the works, such as *The Voyage Out* and *Night and Day*, are still written, to large extent, in the conventional form, yet, even those books have already displayed the embryo of experiment and innovation in the artistic form and technique. *The Voyage Out* can well represent the characteristics of this period. To reflect the growing awareness of the heroine as faithful as possible, the author chooses several "moments of being" which is employed in a more subtle way in her later works. Also in this book, Virginia's language skill in revealing the characters' inner emotional states, including the use of single charged utterance cannot fail to draw a special attention.

At the second stage, Woolf's achievements mainly lie in the creation of innovative fictions of "stream of consciousness". The works, such as: *Jacob's Room* (1922), *Mrs. Dalloway* (1925), *To the Lighthouse* (1927), *The Waves* (1931). Of which the most beautifully written is *To the Lighthouse* as most agree. To express the real interior experience of the characters, the writer employs lots of techniques of "stream of consciousness", the most prominent of which should be multi-personal representation of consciousness. It demonstrates how Virginia Woolf successfully turns completely from the exterior world to the inner world, revealing the novelist's conscious efforts to pursue the interior reality.

At the third stage, Woolf once again displays her spirit of experiment and innovation and her unremitting pursuit for interior reality. The works: *Orlando* (1928), *The Years* (1937), *Between the Acts* (1941), Her biography of *Roger Fry* (1940). She has walked out of the pure "stream of consciousness" fictions and created a synthetic form of art, represented *Between Acts*. Different from *To the Lighthouse* completely and other excellent fictions of "stream of consciousness", which almost focus on what is going on in the characters' consciousness, *Between the Acts* is covered, to a large extent, with the characters' speech. It is just through the demonstration of the fragmentation and ineffectiveness of the language of both the play and the characters that Virginia Woolf manages to convey the fragmentation of modern consciousness and the destructive tension people are caught in.

So it is necessary to appreciate Woolf's major works to understand her feminist ideas and her "stream of consciousness".

5.1 Jacob's Room (1922)

Jacob's Room was written in 1922. In the novel, the time background is set in prewar England. It mainly explains Jacob's own life from the female perspective, from his childhood, Cambridge college time gradually to the adult period. The most of the stories focuses on the London Times. Although he went to Italy tourism, and then to the Greek, traveled the Quartet. However, he finally lost his life in the World War Ⅰ in the end of the novel.

In *Jacob's Room*, the writer does not give readers the traditional story plot, an open room and a shadow like Scabbers to remind Mr. Jacob's public life, around which all activities and emotional reactions expanded. The whole novel consists of a number of fragments of life which have no relations with each other, do not emphasize the description of integrity, so what is left to readers is impressionistic collage. The hero's presence such as his childhood in Scaburo, his Cambridge University time, the Greek tourism, his friendship with Bonano, the emotional entanglement with several women and his final death in the World War Ⅰ is conveyed by other characters' eyes—the mother of Flanders and his friends and strangers he met. The characters appeared and disappeared superficially, which reflected the words "life is just a string of shadow". In this novel, the narrator no longer collected and refined the psychology of the characters, no longer came forward to introduce the environment, the story and the characters' sufferings, but presented the native state of flow of consciousness in people's deep inside directly and disorderly in front of readers. The author almost abandoned all the details of the matter, just in an effort to capture the character's moment of experience, and reveal the characters' inner secret thoughts and unconscious desire. The external action of characters only served as the media to perform his inner mood, so the action itself seemed to have nothing to do with the theme of the novel.

Virginia Woolf always attaches great importance to the relations among the characters, because a character's behavior is usually associated with another character's behavior. Therefore, the characters are always in a kind of "interconnected" structure, which makes it very real. Although *Jacob's Room* is a description of a male's growth; the novel itself is a feminine world; in this world, the role of the father is absent; the only male friend is a gay. As Jacob is only a carrier, floating in the air, he is reflected in the psychology of different women in different period. He is a clue to connect and reflect different women's lives: Mrs. Flanders, the widow lady; Clara, who loves Jacob secretly; Florinda, a prostitutes; and Fanny, a manikin; Sandra, a young wed woman (the second chapter); the scattered people gathered together in a park: James Bonamy in Hyde Park; Clara in a park. When the clock strikes to 5, pregnant clock, in the mind thinking of Jacob; and the same miss Jacob Binhe Road. In this way, the author of the ingenious use of space and time coordinates the juxtaposition of characters and events, previously scattered narrative clues Shoulong, let several rays converge at a point, point to Jacob.

Woolf mainly adopts inner focusing narrative techniques to characterize Jacob, the protagonist. With different characters appearing in the works, the narrative points of view change quickly. For example, in the 13th chapters of the novel, Jacob returned London from Greece. At this time, Woolf arranged him and the others who had close relationship with him to get together through the ingenious arrangements of time and space, in seemly scattered and disordered narrative. At the beginning, Jacob and Bonamy, one of his friends, were sitting in Hyde Park, Clara taking her dog together with Paulie in a park for a walk and calling "Jacob" twice in her heart, but without encountering Jacob himself, at this time, a horse free from the rider was suddenly running. Clara shouted: "Oh, stop it!" Julia Elliot was walking in Hyde Park without seeing Jacob nor meeting Clara, but she also saw the galloping horse. In the scene, the novel marked the time — Julia went to the appointment at 5 o'clock. Mrs. William Congreve, she told her that she must reach the Bruton Street within 12 minutes. Woolf skillfully juxtaposed the characters and events in proper time and space to fold the scattered narrative clues to point to Jacob, so the narrative is put together organically.

Jacob' s Room

(Chapter 13)

The story:

"The Height of the season," said Bonamy.

The sun had already blistered the paint on the backs of the green chairs in Hyde Park; peeled the bark off the plane trees; and turned the earth to powder and to smooth yellow pebbles. Hyde Park was circled, incessantly, by turning wheels.

"The height of the season," said Bonamy sarcastically.

He was sarcastic because of Clara Durrant; because Jacob had come back from Greece very brown and lean, with his pockets full of Greek notes, which he pulled out when the chair man came for pence; because Jacob was silent.

"He has not said a word to show that he is glad to see me," thought Bonamy bitterly.

The motor cars passed incessantly over the bridge of the Serpentine; the upper classes walked upright, or bent themselves gracefully over the palings; the lower classes lay with their knees cocked up, flat on their backs; the sheep grazed on pointed wooden legs; small children ran down the sloping grass, stretched their arms, and fell.

"Very urbane," Jacob brought out.

"Urbane" on the lips of Jacob had mysteriously all the shapeliness of a character which Bonamy thought daily more sublime, devastating, terrific than ever, though he was still, and perhaps would be for ever, barbaric, obscure.

What superlatives! What adjectives! How acquit Bonamy of sentimentality of the grossest sort; of being tossed like a cork on the waves; of having no steady insight into character; of being unsupported by reason, and of drawing no comfort whatever from the works of the classics?

"The height of civilization," said Jacob.

He was fond of using Latin words.

Magnanimity, virtue—such words when Jacob used them in talk with Bonamy meant that he took control of the situation; that Bonamy would play round him like an affectionate spaniel; and that (as likely as not) they would end by rolling on the floor.

"And Greece?" said Bonamy. "The Parthenon and all that?"

"There's none of this European mysticism," said Jacob.

"It's the atmosphere. I suppose," said Bonamy. "And you went to Constantinople?"

"Yes," said Jacob.

Bonamy paused, moved a pebble; then darted in with the rapidity and certainty of a lizard's tongue.

"You are in love!" he exclaimed.

Jacob blushed.

The sharpest of knives never cut so deep.

As for responding, or taking the least account of it, Jacob stared straight ahead of him, fixed, monolithic—oh, very beautiful! —like a British Admiral, exclaimed Bonamy in a rage, rising from his seat and walking off; waiting for some sound; none came; too proud to look back; walking quicker and quicker until he found himself gazing into motor cars and cursing women. Where was the pretty woman's face? Clara's— Fanny's—Florinda's? Who was the pretty little creature?

Not Clara Durrant.

The Aberdeen terrier must be exercised, and as Mr. Bowley was going that very moment—would like nothing better than a walk—they went together, Clara and kind little Bowley—Bowley who had rooms in the Albany, Bowley who wrote letters to the "Times" in a jocular vein about foreign hotels and the Aurora Borealis—Bowley who liked young people and walked down Piccadilly with his right arm resting on the boss of his back.

"Little demon!" cried Clara, and attached Troy to his chain.

Bowley anticipated—hoped for—a confidence. Devoted to her mother, Clara sometimes felt her a little, well, her mother was so sure of herself that she could not understand other people being—being— "as ludicrous as I am," Clara jerked out (the dog tugging her forwards). And Bowley thought she looked like a huntress and turned over in his mind which it should be—some pale virgin with a slip of the moon in her hair, which was a flight for Bowley.

The colour was in her cheeks. To have spoken outright about her mother— still, it was only to Mr. Bowley, who loved her, as everybody must; but to speak was unnatural to her, yet it was awful to feel, as she had done all day, that she must tell someone.

"Wait till we cross the road," she said to the dog, bending down.

Happily she had recovered by that time.

"She thinks so much about England," she said. "She is so anxious–"

Bowley was defrauded as usual. Clara never confided in anyone.

"Why don't the young people settle it, eh?" he wanted to ask. "What's all this about England?" —a question poor Clara could not have answered, since, as Mrs. Durrant discussed with Sir Edgar the policy of Sir Edward Grey, Clara only wondered why the cabinet looked dusty, and Jacob had never come. Oh, here was Mrs. Bowley Johnson . . .

And Clara would hand the pretty china teacups, and smile at the compliment—that no one in London made tea so well as she did.

"We get it at Brocklebank's," she said, "in Cursitor Street."

Ought she not to be grateful? Ought she not to be happy?

Especially since her mother looked so well and enjoyed so much talking to Sir Edgar about Morocco, Venezuela, or some such place.

"Jacob! Jacob!" thought Clara; and kind Mr. Bowley, who was ever so good with old ladies, looked; stopped; wondered whether Elizabeth wasn't too harsh with her daughter; wondered about Bonamy, Jacob—which young fellow was it? —and jumped up directly Clara said she must exercise Troy.

They had reached the site of the old exhibition. They looked at the tulips. Stiff and curled, the little rods of waxy smoothness rose from the earth, nourished yet contained, suffused with scarlet and coral pink. Each had its shadow; each grew trimly in the diamond-shaped wedge as the gardener had planned it.

"Barnes never gets them to grow like that," Clara mused; she sighed.

"You are neglecting your friends," said Bowley, as someone, going the other way, lifted his hat. She started; acknowledged Mr. Lionel Parry's bow; wasted on him what had sprung for Jacob. ("Jacob! Jacob!" she thought.)

"But you'll get run over if I let you go," she said to the dog.

"England seems all right," said Mr. Bowley.

The loop of the railing beneath the statue of Achilles was full of parasols and waistcoats; chains and bangles; of ladies and gentlemen, lounging elegantly, lightly observant.

"This statue was erected by the women of England..." Clara read out with a foolish little laugh. "Oh, Mr. Bowley! Oh!" Gallop-gallop-gallop-a horse galloped past without a rider. The stirrups swung; the pebbles spurted.

"Oh, stop! Stop it, Mr. Bowley!" she cried, white, trembling, gripping his arm, utterly unconscious, the tears coming.

"Tut-tut!" said Mr. Bowley in his dressing room an hour later. "Tut-tut!" —a comment that was profound enough, though inarticulately expressed, since his valet was handing his shirt studs.

Julia Eliot, too, had seen the horse run away, and had risen from her seat to watch the end of the incident, which, since she came of a sporting family, seemed to her slightly ridiculous. Sure enough the little man came pounding behind with his breeches dusty; looked thoroughly annoyed; and was being helped to mount by a policeman when Julia Eliot, with a sardonic smile, turned towards the Marble Arch on her errand of mercy. It was only to visit a sick old lady who had known her mother and perhaps the Duke of Wellington; for Julia shared the love of her sex for the distressed; liked to visit death-beds; threw slippers at weddings; received confidences by the dozen; knew more pedigrees than a scholar knows dates, and was one of the kindliest, most generous, least continent of women.

Yet five minutes after she had passed the statue of Achilles she had the rapt look of one brushing through crowds on a summer's afternoon, when the trees are rustling, the wheels churning yellow, and the tumult of the present seems like an elegy for past youth and past summers, and there rose in her mind a curious sadness, as if time and eternity showed through skirts and waistcoasts, and she saw people passing tragically to destruction. Yet, Heaven knows, Julia was no fool. A sharper woman at a bargain did not exist. She was always punctual. The watch on her wrist gave her twelve minutes and a half in which to reach Bruton Street. Lady Congreve expected her at five.

The gilt clock at Verrey's was striking five.

Florinda looked at it with a dull expression, like an animal. She looked at the clock; looked at the door; looked at the long glass opposite; disposed her cloak; drew closer to the table, for she was pregnant—no doubt about it, Mother Stuart said, recommending remedies, consulting friends; sunk, caught by the heel, as she tripped so lightly over the surface.

Her tumbler of pinkish sweet stuff was set down by the waiter; and she sucked, through a straw, her eyes on the looking-glass, on the door, now soothed by the sweet taste. When Nick Bramham came in it was plain, even to the young Swiss waiter, that there was a bargain between them. Nick hitched his clothes together clumsily; ran his fingers through his hair; sat down, to an ordeal, nervously. She looked at him; and set off laughing; laughed—laughed—laughed. The young Swiss waiter, standing with crossed legs by the pillar, laughed too.

The door opened; in came the roar of Regent Street, the roar of traffic, impersonal, unpitying; and sunshine grained with dirt. The Swiss waiter must see to the newcomers. Bramham lifted his glass.

"He's like Jacob," said Florinda, looking at the newcomer.

"The way he stares." She stopped laughing.

Jacob, leaning forward, drew a plan of the Parthenon in the dust in Hyde Park, a network of strokes at least, which may have been the Parthenon, or again a mathematical diagram. And why was the pebble so emphatically ground in at the corner? It was not to count his notes that he took out a wad of papers and read a long flowing letter which Sandra had written two days ago at Milton Dower House with his book before her and in her mind the memory of something said or attempted, some moment in the dark on the road to the Acropolis which (such was her creed) mattered for ever.

"He is," she mused, "like that man in Moliere."

She meant Alceste. She meant that he was severe. She meant that she could deceive him.

"Or could I not?" she thought, putting the poems of Donne back in the bookcase. "Jacob," she went on, going to the window and looking over the spotted flower-beds across the grass where the piebald cows grazed under beech trees, "Jacob would be shocked."

The perambulator was going through the little gate in the railing. She kissed her hand; directed by the nurse, Jimmy waved his.

"He's a small boy," she said, thinking of Jacob.

And yet—Alceste?

"What a nuisance you are!" Jacob grumbled, stretching out first one leg and then the other and feeling in each trouser-pocket for his chair ticket.

"I expect the sheep have eaten it," he said. "Why do you keep sheep?"

"Sorry to disturb you, sir," said the ticket-collector, his hand deep in the enormous pouch of pence.

"Well, I hope they pay you for it," said Jacob. "There you are. No. You can stick to it. Go and get drunk."

He had parted with half-a-crown, tolerantly, compassionately, with considerable contempt for his species.

Even now poor Fanny Elmer was dealing, as she walked along the Strand, in her incompetent way with this very careless, indifferent, sublime manner he had of talking to railway guards or porters; or Mrs. Whitehorn, when she consulted him about her little boy who was beaten by the schoolmaster.

Sustained entirely upon picture post cards for the past two months, Fanny's idea of Jacob was more statuesque, noble, and eyeless than ever. To reinforce her vision she had taken to visiting the British Museum, where, keeping her eyes downcast until she was alongside of the battered Ulysses, she opened them and got a fresh shock of Jacob's presence, enough to last her half a day. But this was wearing thin. And she wrote now—poems, letters that were never posted, saw his face in advertisements on hoardings, and would cross the road to let the barrel-organ turn her musings to rhapsody. But at breakfast (she shared rooms with a teacher), when the butter was smeared about the plate, and the prongs of the forks were clotted with old egg yolk, she revised these visions violently; was, in truth, very cross; was losing her complexion, as Margery Jackson told her, bringing the whole thing down (as she laced her stout boots) to a level of mother-wit, vulgarity, and sentiment, for she had loved too; and been a fool.

"One's godmothers ought to have told one," said Fanny, looking in at the window of Bacon, the map seller, in the Strand—told one that it is no use making a fuss; this is life, they should have said, as Fanny said it now, looking at the large yellow globe marked with steamship lines.

"This is life, This is life." said Fanny.

"A very hard face," thought Miss Barrett, on the other side of the glass, buying maps of the Syrian desert and waiting impatiently to be served. "Girls look old so soon nowadays."

The equator swam behind tears.

"Piccadilly?" Fanny asked the conductor of the omnibus, and climbed to the top. After all, he would, he must, come back to her.

But Jacob might have been thinking of Rome; of architecture; of jurisprudence; as he sat under the plane tree in Hyde Park.

…

5.2 Mrs. Dalloway (1925)

The novel is set in London in 1923. It describes a mid June day (Wednesday) in the life of an upper-middle class woman, Clarissa Dalloway (51, married with a daughter). She is organizing a party and the reader follows her while she goes shopping in Bond Street (she needs some flowers for the party she is giving in the evening). While she is in the flower shop, a car drives noisily past and shifts the attention on the street where Septimus (a shell-shocked veteran of the war) and Lucrezia Warren Smith (his wife) are walking. Septimus's mental disorder has necessitated the calling in of Sir William Bradshaw, a famous psychiatrist and one of the guests of Mr Dalloway's party. There is no real plot because the novel presents the thoughts, memories, associations and ideas of the characters in a stream of consciousness form. The aim of the book is to carry out an analysis of time and of the endless changing of life.

Clarissa married Richard Dalloway decades after she separated with her first lover Peter Walsh. Richard was a down to earth congressman with a bright future. Though there were gratitude and respect between them, they didn't quite understand each other. Clarissa never knew Richard's love. Clarissa needed straight forward expression of love, but out of laziness or shyness. Richard didn't say, though he bare his love in his heart. Years passed, Clarissa could not forget Peter, who she once and for life long deep in love with. On her way to the flower shop, she thought about Peter; she still remembered exactly every word he had said. When she heard at a concert that Peter had married a woman met on the boat going to India, her heart was torn into pieces. When Peter turned up unexpectedly in her bedroom in the morning when she was to have a party at night, all her emotions of the past was stirred up. In the years when they were together, they understood each other thoroughly. On Clarissa's part, she thought Peter to be a loafer, and asserted that he won't achieve anything in his life. Thus, she rejected Peter, who was so passionately in love with her, and accept Richard's proposal.

The center of Clarissa' s life is the party. It's her way of communication with outside world; it's her temporary escape from loneliness of her inward world; most important of all, she believed that the party would help her husband with his career. When she read from the telephone pad that Lady Bruton invited Mr. Dalloway to lunch without inviting her, feeling been forgotten, her world collapsed. She prepared for the party at that night wholeheartedly, later her thoughtful arrangement proved to be a success. As Peter Walsh expected, Clarissa had become a perfect hostess. Clarissa got satisfaction from her success in parties, though Richard wasn't necessarily benefited from her success. Richard needed Clarissa's love, but Clarissa mistakenly took her efforts to the party which Richard didn't care much.

The novel represents the writer's stream of consciousness. The time is condensed with innumerable memories and imagination. In one way, the book is a random flow of consciousness; in another way, it is an interconnection of the closely related past and present, of physical time and psychological time, of sanity and insanity, of the interior and outside world.

The novel unfolded with its first sentence, "Mrs. Dalloway said she would buy the flowers herself." "What a morning-fresh as if issued to children on a beach", it's Mrs. Dalloway's morning and her day. With the strikes of the Big Ben, we see the day lasted from 9: 00 am to midnight when Mrs. Dalloway's party was over. This fifteen hours record Clarissa's activities including buying flowers, mending dress, meeting Peter, and hosting a party, as well as a war veteran's physical and psychological experience during this day: he was wandering in a cranky and frightened mood as a result of the war terror and he finally committed suicide in fear of the chase of psychologist. It is a day for Mrs. Dalloway, yet a life for Septimus: the physical time of a day represents the psychological time of one's life. These two types of time interweave and their stream of consciousness overlaps. The Big Ben is reporting the exact physical time while every single physical moment is filled with complex consciousness of various characters. This density of time greatly explores the unlimited expansibility and compactness of the stream of consciousness in fiction structure.

Another looseness of the structure finds its representation in the relationship between Mrs. Dalloway and Septimus. They are the most important voices, and their consciousness conceives the spirit of the book. One of the most puzzling aspects of

Mrs. Dalloway is the apparent unconnected nature of these two narratives. The novel follows the central character Clarissa Dalloway, from early morning through to night on a day on which she gives a formal party, then the narration jumps between her story and the more sensational narrative of a shell-shocked war veteran, Septimus Warren Smith, and his eventual suicide. Ostensibly, the two stories are not linked and appear to merge only when Clarissa overhears a guest at her party talking of Septimus's death.

Among the souls, Mrs. Dalloway and Septimus still count most. The essential dialectical struggle in the book is between the opposite adaptations to the world which are represented by Clarissa and by Septimus. The stream of consciousness intensifies while it comes to a struggle between the sanity and insanity, for this two opposite adaptations to the world bring out the deepest thoughts Woolf demonstrates her brilliant capability. Clarissa is complete and sane; the unknown young man is Septimus, a patient suffering from insanity and driven to suicide by the psychologists. He represents the insane looking on the world. His insanity begins after his best friend Evan being killed in the war.

With the interior monologue of Mrs. Dalloway in the novel, the story travels forward and backward in time, and in and out of the characters' minds, to construct a complete image of Clarissa's life and of the post-war social structure in England.

The novel itself is preoccupied with a number of issues. The most obvious are feminism and madness displayed respectively by the two characters Clarissa Dalloway and Septimus Warren Smith. As a commentary on post-war society, Clarissa's character highlights the role of women as supporting members in an English family, which is a different role compared to the old traditional women image in England. However, this role is not perfect either, as many of the women characters in this novel have repressions but are ironically covered by the social masks of their own.

In *Mrs. Dalloway* (1923), Woolf compared two kinds of women who bore absolutely different notions respectively with Clarissa be a traditional victorian woman while Sally be a new woman. Compared with Clarissa, a woman with pure femininity, Sally was a woman with both femininity and masculinity. While Clarissa struggling in her lonely and boring middle age life, Sally enjoys a brilliant life, harmonious marriage and domestic bliss. In this novel, the concept of new women was put forward. And this was the first time when Woolf created a character with both femininity and masculinity in head. The image of Sally is the origin of Woolf's androgynous thought.

Mrs. Dalloway

(The beginning)

(excerpted)

The story:

Mrs. Dalloway said she would buy the flowers herself. For Lucy had her work cut out for her. The doors would be taken off their hinges; Rumpelmayer's men were coming. And then, thought Clarissa Dalloway, what a morning—fresh as if issued to children on a beach.

What a lark! What a plunge! For so it had always seemed to her, when, with a little squeak of the hinges, which she could hear now, she had burst open the French windows and plunged at Bourton into the open air. How fresh, how calm, stiller than this of course, the air was in the early morning; like the flap of a wave; the kiss of a wave; chill and sharp and yet (for a girl of eighteen as she then was) solemn, feeling as she did, standing there at the open window, that something awful was about to happen; looking at the flowers, at the trees with the smoke winding off them and the rooks rising, falling; standing and looking until Peter Walsh said, "Musing among the vegetables?" —was that it? — "I prefer men to cauliflowers" —was that it? He must have said it at breakfast one morning when she had gone out on to the terrace—Peter Walsh. He would be back from India one of these days, June or July, she forgot which, for his letters were awfully dull; it was his sayings one remembered; his eyes, his pocket-knife, his smile, his grumpiness and, when millions of things had utterly vanished—how strange it was! —a few sayings like this about cabbages. She stiffened a little on the kerb, waiting for Durtnall's van to pass. A charming woman, Scrope Purvis thought her (knowing her as one does know people who live next door to one in Westminster); a touch of the bird about her, of the jay, blue-green, light, vivacious, though she was over fifty, and grown very white since her illness. There she perched, never seeing him, waiting to cross, very upright.

For having lived in Westminster—how many years now? Over twenty, —one feels even in the midst of the traffic, or waking at night, Clarissa was positive, a particular hush, or solemnity; an indescribable pause; a suspense (but that might be her heart, affected, they said, by influenza) before Big Ben strikes. There! Out it boomed. First a warning, musical; then the hour, irrevocable. The leaden circles dissolved in the air. Such fools we are, she thought, crossing Victoria Street. For Heaven only knows why one loves it so, how one sees it so, making it up, building it round one, tumbling it, creating it every moment afresh; but the veriest frumps, the most dejected of miseries sitting on doorsteps (drink their downfall) do the same; can't be dealt with, she felt positive, by Acts of Parliament for that very reason: they love life. In people's eyes, in the swing, tramp, and trudge; in the bellow and the uproar; the carriages, motor cars, omnibuses, vans, sandwich men shuffling and swinging; brass bands; barrel organs; in the triumph and the jingle and the strange high singing of some aeroplane overhead was what she loved; life; London; this moment of June for it was the middle of June.

The war was over, except for someone like Mrs. Foxcroft at the Embassy last night eating her heart out because that nice boy was killed and now the old Manor House must go to a cousin; or Lady Bexborough who opened a bazaar, they said, with the telegram in her hand, John, her favourite, killed; but it was over; thank Heaven—over. It was June. The King and Queen were at the Palace. And everywhere, though it was still so early, there was a beating, a stirring of galloping ponies, tapping of cricket bats; Lords, Ascot, Ranelagh and all the rest of it; wrapped in the soft mesh of the grey-blue morning air, which, as the day wore on, would unwind them, and set down on their lawns and pitches the bouncing ponies, whose forefeet just struck the ground and up they sprung, the whirling young men, and laughing girls in their transparent muslins who, even now, after dancing all night, were taking their absurd woolly dogs for a run; and even now, at this hour, discreet old dowagers were shooting out in their motor cars on errands of mystery; and the shopkeepers were fidgeting in their windows with their paste and diamonds, their lovely old sea-green brooches in eighteenth-century settings to tempt Americans (but one must economise, not buy things rashly for Elizabeth), and she, too, owing it as she did with an absurd and faithful passion, being part of it, since her people were courtiers once in the time of the Georges, she, too, was going that very night to kindle and illuminate; to give her party. But how strange, on entering the Park, the silence; the mist; the hum; the slow-swimming happy ducks; the pouched birds waddling; and who should be coming along with his back against the Government buildings, most appropriately, carrying a despatch box stamped with the Royal Arms, who but Hugh Whitbread; her old friend Hugh—the admirable Hugh!

"Good morning to you, Clarissa!" said Hugh, rather extravagantly, for they had known each other as children. "Where are you off to?"

"I love walking in London," said Mrs. Dalloway. "Really it's better than walking in the country."

They had just come up—unfortunately—to see doctors. Other people came to see pictures; go to the opera; take their daughters out; the Whitbreads came "to see doctors." Times without number Clarissa had visited Evelyn Whitbread in a nursing home. Was Evelyn ill again? Evelyn was a good deal out of sorts, said Hugh, intimating by a kind of pout or swell of his very well-covered, manly, extremely handsome, perfectly up-holstered body (he was almost too well dressed always, but presumably had to be, with his little job at Court) that his wife had some internal ailment, nothing serious, which, as an old friend, Clarissa Dalloway would quite understand without requiring him to specify. Ah yes, she did of course; what a nuisance; and felt very sisterly and oddly conscious at the same time of her hat. Not the right hat for the early morning, was that it? For Hugh always made her feel, as he bustled on, raising his hat rather extravagantly and assuring her that she might be a girl of eighteen, and of course he was coming to her party tonight, Evelyn absolutely insisted, only a little late he might be after the party at the Palace to which he had to take one of Jim's boys, —she always felt a little skimpy beside Hugh; schoolgirlish; but attached to him, partly from having known him always, but she did think him a good sort in his own way. She could remember scene after scene at Bourton—Peter furious; Hugh not, of course, his match in any way, but still not a positive imbecile as Peter made out; not a mere barber's block. When his old mother wanted him to give up shooting or to take her to bath he did it, without a word; he was really unselfish, and as for saying, as Peter did, that he had no heart, no brain, nothing but the manners and breeding of an English gentleman, that was only her dear Peter at his worst; and he could be intolerable; he could be impossible; but adorable to walk with on a morning like this. (June had drawn out every leaf on the trees. The mothers of Pimlico gave suck to their young. Messages were passing from the Fleet to the Admiralty. Arlington Street and Piccadilly seemed to chafe the very air in the Park and lift its leaves hotly, brilliantly, on waves of that divine vitality which Clarissa loved. To dance, to ride, she had adored all that.)

For they might be parted for hundreds of years, she and Peter; she never wrote a letter and his were dry sticks; but suddenly it would come over her. If he were with me now what would he say? —some days, some sights bringing him back to her calmly, without the old bitterness; which perhaps was the reward of having cared for people; they came back in the middle of St. James's Park on a fine morning—indeed they did.

But Peter—however beautiful the day might be, and the trees and the grass, and the little girl in pink—Peter never saw a thing of all that. He would put on his spectacles, if she told him to; he would look. It was the state of the world that interested him; Wagner, Pope's poetry, people's characters eternally, and the defects of her own soul. How he scolded her! How they argued! She would marry a Prime Minister and stand at the top of a staircase; the perfect hostess he called her (she had cried over it in her bedroom), she had the makings of the perfect hostess, he said. So she would still find herself arguing in St. James's Park, still making out that she had been right—and she had too—not to marry him. For in marriage a little license, a little independence there must be between people living together day in day out in the same house; which Richard gave her, and she him. (Where was he this morning for instance? Some committee, she never asked what.) But with Peter everything had to be shared; everything gone into. And it was intolerable, and when it came to that scene in the little garden by the fountain, she had to break with him or they would have been destroyed, both of them ruined, she was convinced; though she had borne about with her for years like an arrow sticking in her heart the grief, the anguish; and then the horror of the moment when someone told her at a concert that he had married a woman met on the boat going to India! Never should she forget all that! Cold, heartless, a prude, he called her. Never could she understand how he cared. But those Indian women did presumably silly, pretty, flimsy nincompoops. And she wasted her pity. For he was quite happy, he assured her—perfectly happy though he had never done a thing that they talked of; his whole life had been a failure. It made her angry still. She had reached the Park gates. She stood for a moment looking at the omnibuses in Piccadilly.

...

5.3 To the Lighthouse (1927)

The novel is composed of three parts. In the first part of The Window, the novel is set in the Ramsays' summer home in the Hebrides, on the Isle of Skye. The section begins with Mrs Ramsay assuring James that they should be able to visit the lighthouse on the next day. This prediction is denied by Mr Ramsay, who voices his certainty that the weather will not be clear, an opinion that forces a certain tension between Mr and Mrs Ramsay, and also between Mr Ramsay and James. This particular incident is referred to on various occasions throughout the chapter, especially in the context of Mr and Mrs Ramsay's relationship.

The section closes with a large dinner party. Mr Ramsay nearly snaps at Augustus Carmichael, a visiting poet, when the latter asks for a second serving of soup. Mrs Ramsay, who is striving for the perfect dinner party is herself out of sorts when Paul Rayley and Minta Doyle, two acquaintances whom she has brought together in engagement, arrive late to dinner, as Minta lost her grandmother's brooch on the beach.

The second section of Time Passes is employed by the author to give a sense of time passing. Woolf explained the purpose of this section, writing that it was an interesting experiment [that gave] the sense of ten years passing. This section's role in linking the two dominant parts of the story was also expressed in Woolf's notes for the novel, where above a drawing of an "H" shape she wrote two blocks joined by a corridor. During this period Britain begins and finishes fighting in World War I. In addition, the reader is informed as to the fates of a number of characters introduced in the first part of the novel: Mrs Ramsay passes away, Prue dies from complications of childbirth, and Andrew is killed in the war. Mr Ramsay is left adrift without his wife to praise and comfort him during his bouts of mortal fear and his anguish over doubts regarding his self worth.

In the final section of The Lighthouse, some of the remaining Ramsays return to their summer home ten years after the events of Part I, as Mr Ramsay finally plans on taking the long-delayed trip to the lighthouse with his son James and daughter Camilla. The trip almost doesn't happen, as the children hadn't been ready, but they eventually take off. While they set sail for the lighthouse, Lily attempts to complete her long-unfinished painting. She reconsiders Mrs Ramsay's memory, grateful for her help in pushing Lily to continue with her art, yet at the same time struggling to free herself from the tacit control Mrs Ramsay had over other aspects of her life. Upon finishing the painting and seeing that it satisfies her, she realizes that the execution of her vision is more important to her than the idea of leaving some sort of legacy in her work — a lesson Mr Ramsay has yet to learn.

In *To the Lighthouse* (1927), Virginia Woolf is concerned with exploring the quality and complexity of the relationship between men and women. The novel begins with the controversy about the weather between Mr. Ramsay and Mrs. Ramsay, which indicates that they have different attitudes toward the objects.

Mr. Ramsay and Mrs. Ramsay demonstrate different characteristics respectively: male is pedestrian while female is flexible; men are engaged in social activities, and the topics they often discuss are about academic and politics. However, women must stay at home to look after the children. The binary opposition between male and female here manifests the opposition of culture and nature. Their marriage is the model of a traditional one. It seems very perfect from appearance, but it implies tragedy indeed. Because of the binary opposition, they belong to two different worlds and they cannot understand each other.

Mrs. Ramsay is a typical character of perfect female in the Victorian age. She is beautiful, elegant, warm -hearted, and obedient. Being a good housekeeper, she is the "angle in the house". Mrs. Ramsay devoted all her life to people around her—her husband, eight children and the guests—and the trivial things in her life. She had no time or space for herself until she exhausted to death. In the first part of the novel "The Window", the routine work of her daily life was described as: Reading a story to her son of six; Knitting stockings for the lighthouse keeper's little boy and gathering things like old magazines and some tobacco to amuse the lighthouse keeper whose life on the island was "bored to death"; Going to the town for shopping and visiting a sick woman; Preparing for the party; Accompanying her husband reading and walking in the garden. While giving her love to others, she worn out herself, exhausted to death.

Mr. Ramsay's work includes writing books and teaching philosophy in a college. Being a respectable scholar, he was indulged in thinking about "subject, object and the essence of truth" all day long. Having a logical head, macro and abstract things were his main concern. Under the guidance of reason, Mr. Ramsay came to believe that nothing lasts for ever, including the masterpieces of Shakespeare. In his opinion, "The very stone one kicks with one's boot will outlast Shakespeare." In Mr. Ramsay's head, the world was simplified into a series of facts and his mind was running like a settled program. His stiffly mode of think lacks the support of sense and intuition. Because of that, he could not reach the position of "R", but stuck in position "Q". Thus his career reached a plateau.

Lily, one of the new generations of women, has evident female consciousness. Lily can be seen as a different girl. It is found earlier that Mrs. Ramsay appreciates independence and her self-consciousness in her bolder way expression. Lily in fact is the image of a woman Mrs. Ramsay expects to be of artistic but in vain because the training she accepts has ingrained influence on her behavior.

Compared with Mrs. Ramsay, Lily, though influenced by the convention of the Angel role, struggles to take the individuating process to realize the self. To Lily, the Ramsays marriage is not so perfect as it is thought. Lily hates Mrs. Ramsay's Angel role, which blocks her creation. She unconsciously shows her animus and represses her woman part, fate makes her different from other ladies and restless all the time. Only when she releases her anger and lets her woman characteristic play its part, can she follow her own way of painting and be happy. That is, when she takes the individuating process, she can realize her self.

Being a young woman artist, Lily can be seen as the symbol of the modern woman with new ideas different from the traditional ideas held by Mrs. Ramsay. She does not want to marry and feels clumsy about dealing with other's demands, who hates patriarchal ideology, insists on her own "Being Self" consciousness and at last she reaches "Lighthouse". So Woolf's feminist ideas that the importance of independence for women's development is clearly embodied by the two figures.

From the discussion about *To the Lighthouse*, obviously, the relationship between men and women in the man-centered society is that men are the center of society while women are secondary to men. Virginia Woolf believes that the true relationship between men and women is to make them equal in society. In that situation, the new woman, Lily, tried her best to be herself and pursue her artistic life under the discrimination of male society, which shows Virginia Woolf's embarrassed situation.

To the Lighthouse

(the window)

(Chapter 1)

The story:

"Yes, of course, if it's fine tomorrow," said Mrs Ramsay. "But you'll have to be up with the lark," she added.

To her son these words conveyed an extraordinary joy, as if it were settled, the expedition were bound to take place, and the wonder to which he had looked forward, for years and years it seemed, was, after a night's darkness and a day's sail, within touch. Since he belonged, even at the age of six, to that great clan which cannot keep this feeling separate from that, but must let future prospects, with their joys and sorrows, cloud what is actually at hand, since to such people even in earliest childhood any turn in the wheel of sensation has the power to crystallise and transfix the moment upon which its gloom or radiance rests, James Ramsay, sitting on the floor cutting out pictures from the illustrated catalogue of the Army and Navy stores, endowed the picture of a refrigerator, as his mother spoke, with heavenly bliss. It was fringed with joy. The wheelbarrow, the lawnmower, the sound of poplar trees, leaves whitening before rain, rooks cawing, brooms knocking, dresses rustling—all these were so coloured and distinguished in his mind that he had already his private code, his secret language, though he appeared the image of stark and uncompromising severity, with his high forehead and his fierce blue eyes, impeccably candid and pure, frowning slightly at the sight of human frailty, so that his mother, watching him guide his scissors neatly round the refrigerator, imagined him all red and ermine on the Bench or directing a stern and momentous enterprise in some crisis of public affairs.

"But," said his father, stopping in front of the drawing room window, "it won't be fine."

Had there been an axe handy, a poker, or any weapon that would have gashed a hole in his father's breast and killed him, there and then, James would have seized it. Such were the extremes of emotion that Mr Ramsay excited in his children's breasts by his mere presence; standing, as now, lean as a knife, narrow as the blade of one, grinning sarcastically, not only with the pleasure of disillusioning his son and casting ridicule upon his wife, who was ten thousand times better in every way than he was (James thought), but also with some secret conceit at his own accuracy of judgment. What he said was true. It was always true. He was incapable of untruth; never tampered with a fact; never altered a disagreeable word to suit the pleasure or convenience of any mortal being, least of all of his own children, who, sprung from his loins, should be aware from childhood that life is difficult; facts uncompromising; and the passage to that fabled land where our brightest hopes are extinguished, our frail barks founder in darkness (here Mr Ramsay would straighten his back and narrow his little blue eyes upon the horizon), one that needs, above all, courage, truth, and the power to endure.

"But it may be fine—I expect it will be fine," said Mrs Ramsay, making some little twist of the reddish brown stocking she was knitting, impatiently. If she finished it tonight, if they did go to the Lighthouse after all, it was to be given to the Lighthouse keeper for his little boy, who was threatened with a tuberculous hip; together with a pile of old magazines, and some tobacco, indeed, whatever she could find lying about, not really wanted, but only littering the room, to give those poor fellows, who must be bored to death sitting all day with nothing to do but polish the lamp and trim the wick and rake about on their scrap of garden, something to amuse them. For how would you like to be shut up for a whole month at a time, and possibly more in stormy weather, upon a rock the size of a tennis lawn? she would ask; and to have no letters or newspapers, and to see nobody; if you were married, not to see your wife, not to know how your children were, —if they were ill, if they had fallen down and broken their legs or arms; to see the same dreary waves breaking week after week, and then a dreadful storm coming, and the windows covered with spray, and birds dashed against the lamp, and the whole place rocking, and not be able to put your nose out of doors for fear of being swept in to the sea? How would you like that? she asked, addressing herself particularly to her daughters. So she added, rather differently, one must take them whatever comforts one can. "It's due west," said the atheist Tansley, holding his bony fingers spread so that the wind blew through them, for he was sharing Mr Ramsay's evening walk up and down, up and down the terrace. That is to say, the wind blew from the worst possible direction for landing at the Lighthouse. Yes, he did say disagreeable things, Mrs Ramsay admitted; it was odious of him to rub this in, and make James still more disappointed; but at the same time, she would not let them laugh at him. "The atheist," they called him. "The little atheist," Rose mocked him. Prue mocked him; Andrew, Jasper, Roger mocked him; even old Badger without a tooth in his head had bit him, for being (as Nancy put it) the hundred and tenth young man to chase them all the way up to the Hebrides when it was ever so much nicer to be alone.

"Nonsense," said Mrs Ramsay, with great severity. Apart from the habit of exaggeration which they had from her, and from the implication (which was true) that she asked too many people to stay, and had to lodge some in the town, she could not bear incivility to her guests, to young men in particular, who were poor as churchmice, "Exceptionally able," her husband said, his great admirers, and come there for a holiday. Indeed, she had the whole of the other sex under her protection; for reasons she could not explain, for their chivalry and valour, for the fact that they negotiated treaties, ruled India, controlled finance; finally for an attitude towards herself which no woman could fail to feel or to find agreeable, something trustful, childlike, reverential; which an old woman could take from a young man without loss of dignity, and woe betide the girl—pray Heaven it was none of her daughters! —who did not feel the worth of it, and all that it implied, to the marrow of her bones!

She turned with severity upon Nancy. He had not chased them, she said. He had been asked.

They must find a way out of it all. There might be some simpler way, some less laborious way, she sighed. When she looked in the glass and saw her hair grey, her cheek sunk, at fifty, she thought, possibly she might have managed things better—her husband; money; his books. But for her own part she would never for a single second regret her decision, evade difficulties, or slur over duties. She was now formidable to behold, and it was only in silence, looking up from their plates, after she had spoken so severely about Charles Tansley, that her daughters, Prue, Nancy, Rose—could sport with infidel ideas which they had brewed for themselves of a life different from hers; in Paris, perhaps; a wilder life; not always taking care of some man or other; for there was in all their minds a mute questioning of deference and chivalry, of the Bank of England and the Indian Empire, of ringed fingers and lace, though to them all there was something in this of the essence of beauty, which called out the manliness in their girlish hearts, and made them, as they sat at table beneath their mother's eyes, honour her strange severity, her extreme courtesy, like a queen's raising from the mud to wash a beggar's dirty foot, when she admonished them so very severely about that wretched atheist who had chased them—or, speaking accurately, been invited to stay with them—in the Isle of Skye.

"They'll be no landing at the Lighthouse tomorrow," said Charles Tansley, clapping his hands together as he stood at the window with her husband. Surely, he had said enough. She wished they would both leave her and James alone and go on talking. She looked at him. He was such a miserable specimen, the children said, all humps and hollows. He couldn't play cricket; he poked; he shuffled. He was a sarcastic brute, Andrew said. They knew what he liked best—to be for ever walking up and down, up and down, with Mr Ramsay, and saying who had won this, who had won that, who was a "first rate man" at Latin verses, who was "brilliant but I think fundamentally unsound," who was undoubtedly the "ablest fellow in Balliol", who had buried his light temporarily at Bristol or Bedford, but was bound to be heard of later when his Prolegomena, of which Mr Tansley had the first pages in proof with him if Mr Ramsay would like to see them, to some branch of mathematics or philosophy saw the light of day. That was what they talked about.

She could not help laughing herself sometimes. She said, the other day, something about "waves mountains high". Yes, said Charles Tansley, it was a little rough. "Aren't you drenched to the skin?" she had said. "Damp, not wet through," said Mr Tansley, pinching his sleeve, feeling his socks.

But it was not that they minded, the children said. It was not his face; it was not his manners. It was him—his point of view. When they talked about something interesting, people, music, history, anything, even said it was a fine evening so why not sit out of doors, then what they complained of about Charles Tansley was that until he had turned the whole thing round and made it somehow reflect himself and disparage them—he was not satisfied. And he would go to picture galleries they said, and he would ask one, did one like his tie? God knows, said Rose, one did not.

Disappearing as stealthily as stags from the dinner-table directly the meal was over, the eight sons and daughters of Mr and Mrs Ramsay sought their bedrooms, their fastness in a house where there was no other privacy to debate anything, everything; Tansley's tie; the passing of the Reform Bill; sea birds and butterflies; people; while the sun poured into those attics, which a plank alone separated from each other so that every footstep could be plainly heard and the Swiss girl sobbing for her father who was dying of cancer in a valley of the Grisons, and lit up bats, flannels, straw hats, ink-pots, paint pots, beetles, and the skulls of small birds, while it drew from the long frilled strips of seaweed pinned to the wall a smell of salt and weeds, which was in the towels too, gritty with sand from bathing.

Strife, divisions, difference of opinion, prejudices twisted into the very fibre of being, oh, that they should begin so early, Mrs Ramsay deplored. They were so critical, her children. They talked such nonsense. She went from the dining room, holding James by the hand, since he would not go with the others. It seemed to her such nonsense—inventing differences, when people, heaven knows, were different enough without that. The real differences, she thought, standing by the drawing room window, are enough, quite enough. She had in mind at the moment, rich and poor, high and low; the great in birth receiving from her, half grudging, some respect, for had she not in her veins the blood of that very noble, if slightly mythical, Italian house, whose daughters, scattered about English drawing rooms in the nineteenth century, had lisped so charmingly, had stormed so wildly, and all her wit and her bearing and her temper came from them, and not from the sluggish English, or the cold Scotch; but more profoundly, she ruminated the other problem, of rich and poor, and the things she saw with her own eyes, weekly, daily, here or in London, when she visited this widow, or that struggling wife in person with a bag on her arm, and a note-book and pencil with which she wrote down in columns carefully ruled for the purpose wages and spendings, employment and unemployment, in the hope that thus she would cease to be a private woman whose charity was half a sop to her own indignation, half a relief to her own curiosity, and become what with her untrained mind she greatly admired, an investigator, elucidating the social problem. Insoluble questions they were, it seemed to her, standing there, holding James by the hand. He had followed her into the drawing room, that young man they laughed at; he was standing by the table, fidgeting with something, awkwardly, feeling himself out of things, as she knew without looking round.

They had all gone—the children; Minta Doyle and Paul Rayley; Augustus Carmichael; her husband—they had all gone. So she turned with a sigh and said, "Would it bore you to come with me, Mr Tansley?" She had a dull errand in the town; she had a letter or two to write; it would be ten minutes perhaps; she would put on her hat. And, with her basket and her parasol, there she was again, ten minutes later, giving out a sense of being ready, of being equipped for a jaunt, which, however, she must interrupt for a moment, as they passed the tennis lawn, to ask Mr Carmichael, who was basking with his yellow cat's eyes ajar, so that like a cat's they seemed to reflect the branches moving or the clouds passing, but to give no inkling of any inner thoughts or emotion whatsoever, if he wanted anything.

For they were making the great expedition, she said, laughing. They were going to the town. "Stamps, writing-paper, tobacco?" she suggested, stopping by his side. But no, he wanted nothing. His hands clasped themselves over his capacious paunch, his eyes blinked, as if he would have liked to reply kindly to these blandishments (she was seductive but a little nervous) but could not, sunk as he was in a grey green somnolence which embraced them all, without need of words, in a vast and benevolent lethargy of well-wishing; all the house; all the world; all the people in it, for he had slipped into his glass at lunch a few drops of something, which accounted, the children thought, for the vivid streak of canary-yellow in moustache and beard that were otherwise milk white. No, nothing, he murmured.

He should have been a great philosopher, said Mrs Ramsay, as they went down the road to the fishing village, but he had made an unfortunate marriage. Holding her blackparasol very erect, and moving with an indescribable air of expectation, as if she were going to meet someone round the corner, she told the story; an affair at Oxford with some girl; an early marriage; poverty; going to India; translating a little poetry "very beautifully, I believe," being willing to teach the boys Persian or Hindustanee, but what really was the use of that? —and then lying, as they saw him, on the lawn.

It flattered him; snubbed as he had been, it soothed him that Mrs Ramsay should tell him this. Charles Tansley revived. Insinuating, too, as she did the greatness of man's intellect, even in its decay, the subjection of all wives—not that she blamed the girl, and the marriage had been happy enough, she believed—to their husband's labours, she made him feel better pleased with himself than he had done yet, and he would have liked, had they taken a cab, for example, to have paid the fare.

As for her little bag, might he not carry that? No, no, she said, she always carried that herself. She did too. Yes, he felt that in her. He felt many things, something in particular that excited him and disturbed him for reasons which he could not give. He would like her to see him, gowned and hooded, walking in a procession. A fellowship, a professorship, he felt capable of anything and saw himself—but what was she looking at? At a man pasting a bill. The vast flapping sheet flattened itself out, and each shove of the brush revealed fresh legs, hoops, horses, glistening reds and blues, beautifully smooth, until half the wall was covered with the advertisement of circus; a hundred horsemen, twenty performing seals, lions, tigers... Craning forwards, for she was short-sighted, she read it out... "will visit this town," she read. It was terribly dangerous work for a one-armed man, she exclaimed, to stand on top of a ladder like that—his left arm had been cut off in a reaping machine two years ago.

"Let us all go!" she cried, moving on, as if all those riders and horses had filled her with childlike exultation and made her forget her pity.

"Let's go," he said, repeating her words, clicking them out, however, with a self-consciousness that made her wince. "Let us all go to the circus." No. He could not say it right. He could not feel it right. But why not? She wondered. What was wrong with him then? She liked him warmly, at the moment. Had they not been taken, she asked, to circuses when they were children? Never, he answered, as if she asked the very thing he wanted; She had been longing all these days to say, how they did not go to circuses. It was a large family, nine brothers and sisters, and his father was a working man. "My father is a chemist, Mrs Ramsay. He keeps a shop." He himself had paid his own way since he was thirteen. Often he went without a great coat in winter. He could never "return hospitality" (those were his parched stiff words) at college. He had to make things last twice the time other people did; he smoked the cheapest tobacco; shag; the same the old men did in the quays. He worked hard—seven hours a day; his subject was now the influence of something upon somebody—they were walking on and Mrs Ramsay did not quite catch the meaning, only the words, here and there... dissertation... fellowship... readership... lectureship. She could not follow the ugly academic jargon, that rattled itself off so glibly, but said to herself that she saw now why going to the circus had knocked him off his perch, poor little man, and why he came out, instantly, with all that about his father and mother and brothers and sisters, and she would see to it that they didn't laugh at him any more; she would tell Prue about it. What he would have liked, she supposed, would have been to say how he had gone not to the circus but to Ibsen with the Ramsays. He was an awful prig—oh yes, an insufferable bore. For, though they had reached the town now and were in the main street, with carts grinding past on the cobbles, still he went on talking, about settlements, and teaching, and working men, and helping our own class, and lectures, till she gathered that he had got back entire self-confidence, had recovered from the circus, and was about (and now again she liked him warmly) to tell her—but here, the houses falling away on both sides, they came out on the quay, and the whole bay spread before them and Mrs Ramsay could not help exclaiming, "Oh, how beautiful!" For the great plateful of blue water was before her; the hoary Lighthouse, distant, austere, in the midst; and on the right, as far as the eye could see, fading and falling, in soft low pleats, the green sand dunes with the wild flowing grasses on them, which always seemed to be running away into some moon country, uninhabited of men.

That was the view, she said, stopping, growing grayer-eyed, that her husband loved.

She paused a moment. But now, she said, artists had come here. There indeed, only a few paces off, stood one of them, in Panama hat and yellow boots, seriously, softly, absorbedly, for all that he was watched by ten little boys, with an air of profound contentment on his round red face gazing, and then, when he had gazed, dipping; imbuing the tip of his brush in some soft mound of green or pink. Since Mr Paunceforte had been there, three years before, all the pictures were like that, she said, green and gray, with lemon-coloured sailing-boats, and pink women on the beach.

But her grandmother's friends, she said, glancing discreetly as they passed, took the greatest pains; first they mixed their own colours, and then they ground them, and then they put damp cloths to keep them moist.

So Mr Tansley supposed she meant him to see that that man's picture was skimpy, was that what one said? The colours weren't solid? Was that what one said? Under the influence of that extraordinary emotion which had been growing all the walk, had begun in the garden when he had wanted to take her bag, had increased in the town when he had wanted to tell her everything about himself, he was coming to see himself, and everything he had ever known gone crooked a little. It was awfully strange.

There he stood in the parlour of the poky little house where she had taken him, waiting for her, while she went upstairs a moment to see a woman. He heard her quick step above; heard her voice cheerful, then low; looked at the mats, tea-caddies, glass shades; waited quite impatiently; looked forward eagerly to the walk home; determined to carry her bag; then heard her come out; shut a door; say they must keep the windows open and the doors shut, ask at the house for anything they wanted (she must be talking to a child) when, suddenly, in she came, stood for a moment silent (as if she had been pretending up there, and for a moment let herself be now), stood quite motionless for a moment against a picture of Queen Victoria wearing the blue ribbon of the Garter; when all at once he realized that it was this: it was this: —she was the most beautiful person he had ever seen.

With stars in her eyes and veils in her hair, with cyclamen and wild violets—what nonsense was he thinking? She was fifty at least; she had eight children. Stepping through fields of flowers and taking to her breast buds that had broken and lambs that had fallen; with the stars in her eyes and the wind in her hair—He had

hold of her bag.

"Good-bye, Elsie," she said, and they walked up the street, she holding her parasol erect and walking as if she expected to meet someone round the corner, while for the first time in his life Charles Tansley felt an extraordinary pride; a man digging in a drain stopped digging and looked at her, let his arm fall down and looked at her; for the first time in his life Charles Tansley felt an extraordinary pride; felt the wind and the cyclamen and the violets for he was walking with a beautiful woman. He had hold of her bag.

5.4 Orlando (1928)

The novel *Orlando—Biographer* was a story of miracle, the hero Orlando was also the heroine. He lived over three centuries and had experienced the change from a man to a woman. Orlando was once a nobleman; he was so attractive that even the queen could not resist the temptation of his charm. He accompanied the queen and once was an embassy to Scotland. He used to fall in love with a Russian princess. When he decided to elope with her, the princess abandoned him and went back to her own country on a ship. Orlando then decided to leave the sad place, so he went to Turkey, there, he changed into a beautiful woman after seven days of sleep. As a woman, Orlando went on her journey, after departure with gypsies, she went back to her hometown—England. There, she lived for centuries, but her life had never be complete until she finally found her husband, with whom, she shared a same mutual understanding. Orlando married Marmaduke Bonthrop Shelmerdine, Esquire. After the marriage, she gave birth to a baby boy, and at last completed the poem *The Oak* which she had been writing for three centuries long. And she led a happy life till the present day.

Orlando—Biographer is one of Woolf's best beloved works. In the novel, Woolf puts forward her androgynous thoughts through a legend in which Orlando changed from a man to a woman and lived for more than three centuries. After the magical change, female Orlando keeps the experiences and thoughts of both sexes, and switches her gender identity between the two sexes freely by means of changing her clothes. In virtue of this unique experience, she completes her poem *The Oak* which she had been writing for three centuries, and finally builds her warm family to fulfill her beautiful life. The figuring of Orlando gives Woolf a more explicit profile to her later androgynous thoughts. She emphasizes the significance of thinking in both sexes' mode for writers. And more importantly, she puts forward an ideal solution to deal with the relationship between both sexes.

Since Orlando switched freely between men's and women's outfits, her androgynous life began. Since then, Orlando's form combined the strength of a man and a woman's grace, and she became the most attractive creature in the world. Orlando was now looked like a woman, but her memory as a man didn't vanish. Female Orlando's new role only doubled her life experiences. Orlando kept her hobby when she was a man. She clipped the net trees, read books, and even walked in the street at night searching for adventures. And of course, her new life added her experiences of women. When she was on deck, she enjoyed the priorities of women. The Captain offered her an awning on deck, and at dinner time, provided her with a slice of corned beef. She even received proposal of marriage from some great noblemen. Orlando's androgynous life brought her double joys; she could easily switch her gender identity by changing her dresses, and enjoy the different funs of both sexes.

As a pretty youngster, Orlando had got large eyes which were like drenched violets; his brow was like "the swelling of a marble dome". In the queen's eyes, Orlando had got "a pair of the finest legs that a young nobleman has ever stood upright upon", and he "was the very image of a noble gentleman". Orlando was such a favor of the queen that she named him her Treasurer and Steward, and made him accompany her. Once, the queen even sent him to Scotland as an ambassador. Except for the queen, Orlando had two or three lovers he met while attending entertainment venue of the lower social class and beer house at night. He kept an intimate relationship with them despite of their inferiority. Besides, he even experienced a crazy love with the princess of Russia when he had already been engaged. Nevertheless, being women's favor could not finally bring him good fortune. When the queen saw Orlando kissing a girl in her own eyes, a feeling of treachery led her to death. When Orlando decided to elope with the princess of Russia, she abandoned him. As a male, Orlando experienced treachery and abandonment despite of his attraction to the opposite sex; he remained single in the end.

After Orlando changed into a female, she experienced the new world of women,

and at the same time, she didn't abandon the things he did when she was a man. She switched between the two sexes, and during these switches, dresses helped him a lot. While reading and receiving clients, she would pick a Chinese style robe of ambiguous gender; And she choose knee-breeches for clipping the net trees, for this was work for men; Then she would choose womanly flowered taffeta to have a drive and receive proposal of marriage from some great noblemen; What's more, she would take a snuff-colored gown like a lawyer's to visit the court and hear her cases; Finally, she would search for adventure in streets at night in a nobleman's outfit. In a man's outfit, she did what men did, clipping trees and searching for adventures; while in women's dress, she received nobleman's proposals. Dress decided Orlando's identity, and decided what she did.

Orlando had been crazy for literature since she was a youngster of sixteen or seventeen. At this early age, Orlando had completed more than fifty-seven poems. Among all his works, *The Oak*, a poem, was his favor. The poem accompanied her from a man to a woman, from a youth to a grown-up. She didn't abandon this poem even when she was in deep depression. When he was a man, he suffered from the satire from Nicholas to whom he much admired. This blow depressed him a lot that he burnt all his poems except *The Oak*. Orlando grew with the poem. When she finally find her androgynous life and enjoyed the double joys brought by her two gender identities, she completed her poem which she had been writing for more than three centuries. So Orlando's androgynous head led her to the accomplishments in both career and marriage.

From the novel, we can get the conclusion that different from liberal feminists, Marxist feminists, socialist feminists or radical feminists, under the same subject of feminism, Woolf has set up her own thoughts. In her opinion, feminism is not necessarily one sex win over the other, but the two sexes live harmoniously together. A woman should bear a man's head in her brain, so that she could understand a man's thought and behavior; On the contrary, a man should bear a woman's head in his brain, so as to understand the woman's thought and behavior like Orlando's situation. This kind of binary thoughts makes the communication between both sexes possible. People with binary thoughts in mind act better than those with single thought, and they also lead better lives than latter ones. This is Woolf's well-known androgynous theory.

Orlando—Biographer

(Chapter 6)

(excerpted)

The story:

Orlando went indoors. It was completely still. It was very silent. There was the ink pot; there was the pen; there was the manuscript of her poem, broken off in the middle of a tribute to eternity. She had been about to say, when Basket and Bartholomew interrupted with the tea things, nothing changes. And then, in the space of three seconds and a half, everything had changed—she had broken her ankle, fallen in love, married Shelmerdine.

There was the wedding ring on her finger to prove it. It was true that she had put it there herself before she met Shelmerdine, but that had proved worse than useless. She now turned the ring round and round, with superstitious reverence, taking care lest it should slip past the joint of her finger.

'The wedding ring has to be put on the third finger of the left hand,' she said, like a child cautiously repeating its lesson, 'for it to be of any use at all.'

She spoke thus, aloud and rather more pompously than was her wont, as if she wished someone whose good opinion she desired to overhear her. Indeed, she had in mind, now that she was at last able to collect her thoughts, the effect that her behaviour would have had upon the spirit of the age. She was extremely anxious to be informed whether the steps she had taken in the matter of getting engaged to Shelmerdine and marrying him met with its approval. She was certainly feeling more herself. Her finger had not tingled once, or nothing to count, since that night on the moor. Yet, she could not deny that she had her doubts. She was married, true; but if one's husband was always sailing round Cape Horn, was it marriage? If one liked him, was it marriage? If one liked other people, was it marriage? And finally, if one still wished, more than anything in the whole world, to write poetry, was it marriage? She had her doubts.

But she would put it to the test. She looked at the ring. She looked at the ink pot. Did she dare? No, she did not. But she must. No, she could not. What should she do then? Faint, if possible. But she had never felt better in her life.

'Hang it all!' she cried, with a touch of her old spirit. 'Here goes!'

And she plunged her pen neck deep in the ink. To her enormous surprise, there was no explosion. She drew the nib out. It was wet, but not dripping. She wrote. The words were a little long in coming, but come they did. Ah! But did they make sense? She wondered, a panic coming over her lest the pen might have been at some of its involuntary pranks again. She read, and then I came to a field where the springing grass was dulled by the hanging cups of fritillaries, sullen and foreign-looking, the snaky flower, scarfed in dull purple, like Egyptian girls:

As she wrote she felt some power (remember we are dealing with the most obscure manifestations of the human spirit) reading over her shoulder, and when she had written 'Egyptian girls', the power told her to stop. Grass, the power seemed to say, going back with a ruler such as governesses use to the beginning, is all right; the hanging cups of fritillaries—admirable; the snaky flower—a thought, strong from a lady's pen, perhaps, but words worth no doubt, sanctions it; but—girls? Are girls necessary? You have a husband at the cape, you say? Ah, well, they'll do.

And so the spirit passed on.

Orlando now performed in spirit (for all this took place in spirit) a deep obeisance to the spirit of her age, such as—to compare great things with small—a traveller, conscious that he has a bundle of cigars in the corner of his suitcase, makes to the customs officer who has obligingly made a scribble of white chalk on the lid. For she was extremely doubtful whether, if the spirit had examined the contents of her mind carefully, it would not have found something highly contraband for which she would have had to pay the full fine. She had only escaped by the skin of her teeth. She had just managed, by some dexterous deference to the spirit of the age, by putting on a ring and finding a man on a moor, by loving nature and being no satirist, cynic, or psychologist—any one of which goods would have been discovered at once—to pass its examination successfully. And she heaved a deep sigh of relief, as, indeed, well she might, for the transaction between a writer and the spirit of the age is one of infinite delicacy, and upon a nice arrangement between the two the whole fortune of his works depends. Orlando had so ordered it that she was in an extremely happy position; she need neither fight her age, nor submit to it; she was of it, yet remained herself. Now, therefore, she could write, and write she did. She wrote. She wrote. She wrote.

It was now November. After November, comes December. Then January, February, March, and April. After April comes May. June, July, August follow. Next is September. Then October, and so, behold, here we are back at November again, with a whole year accomplished. This method of writing biography, though it has its merits, is a little bare, perhaps, and the reader, if we go on with it, may complain that he could recite the calendar for himself and so save his pocket whatever sum the Hogarth Press may think proper to charge for this book. But what can the biographer do when his subject has put him in the predicament into which Orlando has now put us? Life, it has been agreed by everyone whose opinion is worth consulting, is the only fit subject for novelist or biographer; life, the same authorities have decided, has nothing whatever to do with sitting still in a chair and thinking. Thought and life are as the poles as under. Therefore—since sitting in a chair and thinking is precisely what Orlando is doing now—there is nothing for it but to recite the calendar, tell one's beads, blow one's nose, stir the fire, look out of the window, until she has done. Orlando sat so still that you could have heard a pin drop. Would, indeed, that a pin had dropped! That would have been life of a kind. Or if a butterfly had fluttered through the window and settled on her chair, one could write about that. Or suppose she had got up and killed a wasp. Then, at once, we could out with our pens and write. For there would be blood shed, if only the blood of a wasp. Where there is blood there is life. And if killing a wasp is the merest trifle compared with killing a man, still it is a fitter subject for novelist or biographer than this mere wool-gathering; this thinking; this sitting in a chair day in, day out, with a cigarette and a sheet of paper and a pen and an ink pot. If only subjects, we might complain (for our patience is wearing thin), had more consideration for their biographers! What is more irritating than to see one's subject, on whom one has lavished so much time and trouble, slipping out of one's grasp altogether and indulging—witness her sighs and gasps, her flushing, her palings, her eyes now bright as lamps, now haggard as dawns—what is more humiliating than to see all this dumb show of emotion and excitement gone through before our eyes when we know that what causes it—thought and imagination—are of no importance whatsoever?

But Orlando was a woman—Lord Palmerston had just proved it. And when we are writing the life of a woman, we may, it is agreed, waive our demand for action, and substitute love instead. Love, the poet has said, is woman's whole existence. And if we look for a moment at Orlando writing at her table, we must admit that never was there a woman more fitted for that calling. Surely, since she is a woman, and a beautiful woman, and a woman in the prime of life, she will soon give over this pretense of writing and thinking and begin at least to think of a gamekeeper (and as

long as she thinks of a man, nobody objects to a woman thinking). And then she will write him a little note (and as long as she writes little notes nobody objects to a woman writing either) and make an assignation for Sunday dusk and Sunday dusk will come; and the gamekeeper will whistle under the window—all of which is, of course, the very stuff of life and the only possible subject for fiction. Surely Orlando must have done one of these things. Alas, —a thousand times, alas, Orlando did none of them. Must it then be admitted that Orlando was one of those monsters of iniquity who do not love? She was kind to dogs, faithful to friends, generosity itself to a dozen starving poets, had a passion for poetry. But love—as the male novelists define it—and who, after all, speak with greater authority? —has nothing whatever to do with kindness, fidelity, generosity, or poetry. Love is slipping off one's petticoat and—But we all know what love is. Did Orlando do that? Truth compels us to say no; she did not. If then, the subject of one's biography will neither love nor kill, but will only think and imagine, we may conclude that he or she is no better than a corpse and so leave her.

The only resource now left us is to look out of the window. There were sparrows; there were starlings; there were a number of doves, and one or two rooks, all occupied after their fashion. One finds a worm; another a snail. One flutters to a branch; another takes a little run on the turf. Then a servant crosses the courtyard, wearing a green baize apron. Presumably he is engaged on some intrigue with one of the maids in the pantry, but as no visible proof is offered us, in the courtyard, we can but hope for the best and leave it. Clouds pass, thin or thick, with some disturbance of the colour of the grass beneath. The sun-dial registers the hour in its usual cryptic way. One's mind begins tossing up a question or two, idly, vainly, about this same life. Life, it sings, or croons rather, like a kettle on a hob. Life, life, what art thou? Light or darkness, the baize apron of the under-footman or the shadow of the starling on the grass?

Let us go, then, exploring, this summer morning, when all are adoring the plum blossom and the bee. And humming and hawing, let us ask of the starling (who is a more sociable bird than the lark) what he may think on the brink of the dustbin, whence he picks among the sticks combings of scullion's hair. What's life, we ask, leaning on the farm yard gate; Life, Life, Life! cries the bird, as if he had heard, and knew precisely, what we meant by this bothering prying habit of ours of asking questions indoors and out and peeping and picking at daisies as the way is of writers when they don't know what to say next. Then they come here, says the bird, and ask me what life is; Life, Life, Life!

We trudge on then by the moor path, to the high brow of the wine-blue purple-dark hill, and fling ourselves down there, and dream there and see there a grasshopper, carting back to his home in the hollow, a straw. And he says (if sawings like his can be given a name so sacred and tender) Life's labour, or so we interpret the whirr of his dust-choked gullet. And the ant agrees and the bees, but if we lie here long enough to ask the moths, when they come at the evening, stealing among the paler heather bells, they will breathe in our ears such wild nonsense as one hears from telegraph wires in snow storms; tee hee, haw haw. Laughter, Laughter! the moths say.

Having asked then of man and of bird and the insects, for fish, men tell us, who have lived in green caves, solitary for years to hear them speak, never, never say, and so perhaps know what life is—having asked them all and grown no wiser, but only older and colder (for did we not pray once in a way to wrap up in a book something so hard, so rare, one could swear it was life's meaning?) back we must go and say straight out to the reader who waits a tiptoe to hear what life is—alas, we don't know.

At this moment, but only just in time to save the book from extinction, Orlando pushed away her chair, stretched her arms, dropped her pen, came to the window, and exclaimed, 'Done!'

She was almost felled to the ground by the extraordinary sight which now met her eyes. There was the garden and some birds. The world was going on as usual. All the time she was writing the world had continued. 'And if I were dead, it would be just the same!' she exclaimed.

Such was the intensity of her feelings that she could even imagine that she had suffered dissolution, and perhaps some faintness actually attacked her. For a moment she stood looking at the fair, indifferent spectacle with staring eyes. At length she was revived in a singular way. The manuscript which reposed above her heart began shuffling and beating as if it were a living thing, and, what was still odder, and showed how fine a sympathy was between them, Orlando, by inclining her head, could make out what it was that it was saying. It wanted to be read. It must be read. It would die in her bosom if it were not read. For the first time in her life she turned with violence against nature. Elk-hounds and rose bushes were about her in profusion. But elk-hounds and rose bushes can none of them read. It is a lamentable oversight on the part of Providence which had never struck her before. Human beings alone are thus gifted. Human beings had become necessary. She rang the bell. She ordered the carriage to take her to London at once.

"There's just time to catch the eleven forty five, My Lady," said Basket. Orlando had not yet realized the invention of the steam engine, but such was her absorption in the sufferings of a being, who, though not herself, yet entirely depended on her, that she saw a railway train for the first time, took her seat in a railway carriage, and had the rug arranged about her knees without giving a thought to that stupendous invention, which had (the historians say) completely changed the face of Europe in the past twenty years (as, indeed, happens much more frequently than historians suppose). She noticed only that it was extremely smutty; rattled horribly; and the windows stuck. Lost in thought, she was whirled up to London in something less than an hour and stood on the platform at Charing Cross, not knowing where to go.

The old house at Blackfriars, where she had spent so many pleasant days in the eighteenth century, was now sold, part to the Salvation Army, part to an umbrella factory. She had bought another in Mayfair which was sanitary, convenient, and in the heart of the fashionable world, but was it in Mayfair that her poem would be relieved of its desire? Pray God, she thought, remembering the brightness of their ladyships' eyes and the symmetry of their lordship's legs, they haven't taken to reading there.

For that would be a thousand pities. Then there was Lady R.'s. The same sort of talk would be going on there still, she had no doubt. The gout might have shifted from the General's left leg to his right, perhaps. Mr L. might have stayed ten days with R. instead of T. Then Mr Pope would come in. Oh! But Mr Pope was dead. Who were the wits now, she wondered—but that was not a question one could put to a porter, and so she moved on. Her ears were now distracted by the jingling of innumerable bells on the heads of innumerable horses. Fleets of the strangest little boxes on wheels were drawn up by the pavement. She walked out into the Strand. There the uproar was even worse. Vehicles of all sizes, drawn by blood horses and by dray horses, conveying one solitary dowager or crowded to the top by whiskered men in silk hats, were inextricably mixed. Carriages, carts, and omnibuses seemed to her eyes, so long used to the look of a plain sheet of foolscap, alarmingly at loggerheads; and to her ears, attuned to a pen scratching, the uproar of the street sounded violently and hideously cacophonous. Every inch of the pavement was crowded. Streams of people, threading in and out between their own bodies and the lurching and lumbering traffic with incredible agility, poured incessantly east and west. Along the edge of the pavement stood men, holding out trays of toys, and bawled. At corners, women sat beside great baskets of spring flowers and bawled. Boys running in and out of the horses' noses, holding printed sheets to their bodies, bawled too. Disaster! Disaster! At first Orlando supposed that she had arrived at some moment of national crisis; but whether it was happy or tragic, she could not tell. She looked anxiously at people's faces. But that confused her still more. Here would come by a man sunk in despair, muttering to himself as if he knew some terrible sorrow. Past him would nudge a fat, jolly-faced fellow, shouldering his way along as if it were a festival for all the world. Indeed, she came to the conclusion that there was neither rhyme nor reason in any of it. Each man and each woman was bent on his own affairs. And where was she to go?

…

5.5 The Waves (1931)

In *The Waves*, Woolf designed three men and three women as main characters, their colorful lives reflect the six different kinds of life experiences. Bernard is the main character throughout the book; he believes there are something unpleasant and powerless in one's life, but life is still beautiful. He thinks everyone is the creator of life, and not the fate of slaves, so he is always in a peaceful state of mind in facing anything. Rhoda's life is in bright contrast to Bernard's. She was pessimistic, timid and somewhat mysterious. Neville is advocating, rational, rigorous pursuit of knowledge. He likes literature and firmly goes his own way with their own creed. He actively changes himself to adapt to the continuous changes in the social life and desires to experience the essence of life. Louis is very traditional, smart and quick thinking, but gives up his studies because of family reasons. The gap between the reality and the ideal make him unhappy all the life. Susan is tired of the noisy and vanity city life, longing for the pastoral life close to nature; she is a good wife and lovingly mother. Her self-confidence, optimism, strong mindedness leave her a

happy life. Jenny is rich in emotion, desires to stand out of all the girls and becomes the object of attention, so her life is of self-confidence and optimistic. The novel consists of a series of monologues of six friends, occurring at various times in their lives, beginning in childhood, and grouped into eight sections. In the ninth and final section, one of the six, Bernard, seeks to weave their various experiences and personalities into a final unity.

After having got a peak stream of consciousness in *To the Lighthouse*, Woolf goes after extremity. *Mrs. Dalloway* and *To the Lighthouse* have their intensities both in the structure and theme, yet *The Waves* is a poem in the look of a novel. It has nine episodes, each signified by the different period of the sun and signifying the different period of life. The six characters reveal their childhood experience and thought as the sun first rises, then they grow into early adolescence in mid-morning, and adulthood in late morning. When the sun approaches midday position, they reunite to see Percival off to India, but each appears alone. Percival is their hero; he is the silent force around which the group gravitates and rotates, but he is gone at the end of the episode. It comes the noon when the sun lies straight above casting no shadows, but Percival's death leaves everybody sorrow, but Bernard gets a son. The sun's rays begin to slant, but life is monotonous and begins to have no meaning. Life and its discontent approach the end while evening draws upon, and Bernard is last to speak. He spends the remainder text summing up his life and those of the others. Bernard takes on death and the waves crash on the shore.

In *The Waves*, the experiment of the time pattern is carried a step further; indeed, we are going back to morning-to-night, but unlike *Mrs. Dalloway*, a life time from birth to death is gradually described rather than remembered or imagined. It presents us with six characters who grow up from children to men and women, but who never, in the novel, talk to one another, never attain an effective relationship, but move in and out as in the intricate steps of the ballet. The changing emotions and sensations of six parallel lifetimes are setting against the process of a solar day. When "the sun had not yet risen", "the sea was indistinguishable from the sky" like the children vaguely feel the sound and color, their thought and character yet indistinguishable.

The nine episodes which present the lives of the six characters are each preceded by an interlude containing descriptions of nature marking the passing of one day from dawn to dusk. Two natural cycles—birth to death, and dawn to dusk—overlap and form the boundaries of the novel which has not got any other ordering principle. The position of the sun defines the trajectory of the narration. This is more visible in the interludes where this image precedes the nature description. Formally, the interludes are separated from the monologues, but they are integrated into the sequence of soliloquies chiefly through their style and imagery, and therefore the course of the sun parallels the characters' lives.

The framework of the natural cycle has certain traits and produces certain effects which impose order on the material. The perception of imagist and the stream of consciousness is set under this style.

Woolf here makes an emphasis on the essences of personality and inner level of experience. If we say *Mrs. Dalloway* and *To the Lighthouse* get a balance between the outer and inner levels of experience, then *The Waves* is a single road towards souls without parallels. It's a symphony of an only theme and tune, but by a set of instruments.

The Waves is said to be a novel closest to poetry. So it is not surprising to find this novel is permeated with symbolic images which are rich in poetry. Among the many symbolic images, the image of waves is a major one. The waves gather forces and shapes at first, rise to a crest, then break up, and finally dissolve in a thin spread of foam. On the daytime, the waves sparkle and blaze gold under the sunshine. But they lose their gorgeousness when the sun sinks. Dusky sea and darkened sky become indistinguishable, and decayed leaves and frail cargo float on the oozy surface of the sea. This is the image of waves. The form of waves symbolizes the form of human life which is composed of birth, childhood, adolescence, youth, adulthood, old age and death. The wave is a part of nature. So the life-and-death cycle is a part of nature, too. Thus, the wave becomes a symbol of the eternality of the life-and-death cycle.

The Waves

(the last episode)

(excerpted)

The story:

Now the sun had sunk. Sky and sea were indistinguishable. The waves breaking spread their white fans far out over the shore, sent white shadows into the recesses of sonorous caves and then rolled back sighing over the shingle.

The tree shook its branches and a scattering of leaves fell to the ground. There they settled with perfect composure on the precise spot where they would await dissolution. Black and grey were shot into the garden from the broken vessel that had once held red light. Dark shadows blackened the tunnels between the stalks. The thrush was silent and the worm sucked itself back into its narrow hole. Now and again a whitened and hollow straw was blown from an old nest and fell into the dark grasses among the rotten apples. The light had faded from the tool-house wall and the adder's skin hung from the nail empty. All the colours in the room had overflown their banks. The precise brush stroke was swollen and lop-sided; cupboards and chairs melted their brown masses into one huge obscurity. The height from floor to ceiling was hung with vast curtains of shaking darkness. The looking-glass was pale as the mouth of a cave shadowed by hanging creepers.

The substance had gone from the solidity of the hills. Travelling lights drove a plumy wedge among unseen and sunken roads, but no lights opened among the folded wings of the hills, and there was no sound save the cry of a bird seeking some lonelier trees. At the cliff's edge there was an equal murmur of air that had been brushed through forests, of water that had been cooled in a thousand glassy hollows of mid-ocean.

As if there were waves of darkness in the air, darkness moved on, covering houses, hills, trees, as waves of water wash round the sides of some sunken ship. Darkness washed down streets, eddying round single figures, engulfing them; blotting out couples clasped under the showery darkness of elm trees in full summer foliage. Darkness rolled its waves along grassy rides and over the wrinkled skin of the turf, enveloping the solitary thorn tree and the empty snail shells at its foot. Mounting higher, darkness blew along the bare upland slopes, and met the fretted and abraded pinnacles of the mountain where the snow lodges for ever on the hard rock even when the valleys are full of running streams and yellow vine leaves, and girls, sitting on verandahs, look up at the snow, shading their faces with their fans. Them, too, darkness covered.

"Now to sum up," said Bernard. "Now to explain to you the meaning of my life. Since we do not know each other (though I met you once, I think, on board a ship going to Africa), we can talk freely. The illusion is upon me that something adheres for a moment, has roundness, weight, depth, is completed. This, for the moment, seems to be my life. If it were possible, I would hand it to you entire. I would break it off as one breaks off a bunch of grapes. I would say,'Take it. This is my life.'"

But unfortunately, what I see (this globe, full of figures) you do not see. You see me, sitting at a table opposite you, a rather heavy, elderly man, grey at the temples. You see me take my napkin and unfold it. You see me pour myself out a glass of wine. And you see behind me the door opening, and people passing. But in order to make you understand, to give you my life, I must tell you a story—and there are so many, and so many—stories of childhood, stories of school, love, marriage, death, and so on; and none of them are true. Yet like children we tell each other stories, and to decorate them we make up these ridiculous, flamboyant, beautiful phrases. How tired I am of stories, how tired I am of phrases that come down beautifully with all their feet on the ground! Also, how I distrust neat designs of life that are drawn upon half-sheets of note-paper. I begin to long for some little language such as lovers use, broken words, inarticulate words, like the shuffling of feet on the pavement. I begin to seek some design more in accordance with those moments of humiliation and triumph that come now and then undeniably. Lying in a ditch on a stormy day, when it has been raining, then enormous clouds come marching over the sky, tattered clouds, wisps of cloud. What delights me then is the confusion, the height, the indifference and the fury. Great clouds always changing, and movement; something sulphurous and sinister, bowled up, helter-skelter; towering, trailing, broken off, lost, and I forgotten, minute, in a ditch. Of story, of design, I do not see a trace then.

But meanwhile, while we eat, let us turn over these scenes as children turn over the pages of a picture-book and the nurse says, pointing: "That's a cow. That's a boat." Let us turn over the pages, and I will add, for your amusement, a comment in the margin.

"In the beginning, there was the nursery, with windows opening on to a garden, and beyond that the sea. I saw something brighten—no doubt the brass handle of a cupboard. Then Mrs Constable raised the sponge above her head, squeezed it, and out shot, right, left, all down the spine, arrows of sensation. And so, as long as we draw breath, for the rest of time, if we knock against a chair, a table, or a woman, we are pierced with arrows of sensation—if we walk in a garden, if we drink this wine. Sometimes indeed, when I pass a cottage with a light in the window where a child has been born, I could implore them not to squeeze the sponge over that new body. Then, there was the garden and the canopy of the currant leaves which seemed to enclose everything; flowers, burning like sparks upon the depths of green; a rat wreathing with maggots under a rhubarb leaf; the fly going buzz, buzz, buzz upon the nursery ceiling, and plates upon plates of innocent bread and butter. All these things happen in one second and last for ever. Faces loom. Dashing round the corner. "Hello," one says, "there's Jinny. That's Neville. That's Louis in grey flannel with a snake belt. That's Rhoda." She had a basin in which she sailed petals of white flowers. It was Susan who cried, that day when I was in the tool-house with Neville; and I felt my indifference melt. Neville did not melt. "Therefore," I said, "I am myself, not Neville", a wonderful discovery. Susan cried and I followed her. Her wet pocket-handkerchief, and the sight of her little back heaving up and down like a pump-handle, sobbing for what was denied her, screwed my nerves up. "That is not to be borne," I said, as I sat beside her on the roots that were hard as skeletons. I then first became aware of the presence of those enemies who change, but are always there; the forces we fight against. To let oneself be carried on passively is unthinkable. "That's your course, world," one says, "mine is this." So, "Let's explore," I cried, and jumped up, and ran downhill with Susan and saw the stable-boy clattering about the yard in great boots. Down below, through the depths of the leaves, the gardeners swept the lawns with great brooms. The lady sat writing. Transfixed, stopped dead, I thought, "I cannot interfere with a single stroke of those brooms. They sweep and they sweep. Nor with the fixity of that woman writing." It is strange that one cannot stop gardeners sweeping nor dislodge a woman. There they have remained all my life. It is as if one had woken in Stonehenge surrounded by a circle of great stones, these enemies, these presences. Then a wood-pigeon flew out of the trees. And being in love for the first time, I made a phrase—a poem about a wood-pigeon—a single phrase, for a hole had been knocked in my mind, one of those sudden transparencies through which one sees everything. Then more bread and butter and more flies droning round the nursery ceiling on which quivered islands of light, ruffled, opalescent, while the pointed fingers of the lustre dripped blue pools on the corner of the mantelpiece. Day after day as we sat at tea we observed these sights.

"But we were all different. The wax—the virginal wax that coats the spine melted in different patches for each of us. The growl of the boot-boy making love to the tweeny among the gooseberry bushes; the clothes blown out hard on the line; the dead man in the gutter; the apple tree, stark in the moonlight; the rat swarming with maggots; the lustre dripping blue—our white wax was streaked and stained by each of these differently. Louis was disgusted by the nature of human flesh; Rhoda by our cruelty; Susan could not share; Neville wanted order; Jinny love; and so on. We suffered terribly as we became separate bodies." Yet I was preserved from these excesses and have survived many of my friends. I am a little stout, grey, rubbed on the thorax as it were, because it is the panorama of life, seen not from the roof, but from the third-storey window, that delights me, not what one woman says to one man, even if that man is myself. How could I be bullied at school therefore? How could they make things hot for me? There was the Doctor lurching into chapel, as if he trod a battleship in a gale of wind, shouting out his commands through a megaphone, since people in authority always become melodramatic—I did not hate him like Neville, or revere him like Louis. I took notes as we sat together in chapel. There were pillars, shadows, memorial brasses, boys scuffling and swopping stamps behind Prayer Books; the sound of a rusty pump; the Doctor booming, about immortality and quitting ourselves like men; and Percival scratching his thigh. I made notes for stories; drew portraits in the margin of my pocket-book and thus became still more separate. Here are one or two of the figures I saw.

"Percival sat staring straight ahead of him that day in chapel. He also had a way of flicking his hand to the back of his neck. His movements were always remarkable. We all flicked our hands to the backs of our heads—unsuccessfully. He had the kind of beauty which defends itself from any caress. As he was not in the least precocious, he read whatever was written up for our edification without any comment, and thought with that magnificent equanimity (Latin words come naturally) that was to preserve him from so many meannesses and humiliations, that Lucy's flaxen pigtails and pink cheeks were the height of female beauty. Thus preserved, his taste later was of extreme fineness. But there should be music, some wild carol. Through the window should come a hunting—song from some rapid unapprehended life—a sound that shouts among the hills and dies away. What is startling, what is unexpected, what we cannot account for, what turns symmetry to nonsense—that comes suddenly to my mind, thinking of him. The little apparatus of observation is unhinged. Pillars go down; the Doctor floats off; some sudden exaltation possesses me. He was thrown, riding in a race, and when I came along Shaftesbury Avenue tonight, those insignificant and scarcely formulated faces that bubble up out of the doors of the

Tube, and many obscure Indians, and people dying of famine and disease, and women who have been cheated, and whipped dogs and crying children—all these seemed to me bereft. He would have done justice. He would have protected. About the age of forty, he would have shocked the authorities. No lullaby has ever occurred to me capable of singing him to rest.

But let me dip again and bring up in my spoon another of these minute objects which we call optimistically, "characters of our friends" —Louis. He sat staring at the preacher. His being seemed conglobulated in his brow, his lips were pressed; his eyes were fixed, but suddenly they flashed with laughter. Also he suffered from chilblains, the penalty of an imperfect circulation. Unhappy, unfriended, in exile he would sometimes, in moments of confidence, describe how the surf swept over the beaches of his home. The remorseless eye of youth fixed itself upon his swollen joints. Yes, but we were also quick to perceive how cutting, how severe he was, how naturally, when we lay under the elm trees pretending to watch cricket, we waited his approval, seldom given. His ascendancy was resented, as Percival's was adored. Prim, suspicious, lifting his feet like a crane, there was yet a legend that he had smashed a door with his naked fist. But his peak was too bare, too stony for that kind of mist to cling to it. He was without those simple attachments by which one is connected with another. He remained aloof; enigmatic; a scholar capable of that inspired accuracy which has something formidable about it. My phrases (how to describe the moon) did not meet with his approval. On the other hand, he envied me to the point of desperation for being at my ease with servants. Not that the sense of his own deserts failed him. That was commensurate with his respect for discipline. Hence his success, finally, his life, though, was not happy. But look—his eye turns white as he lies in the palm of my hand. Suddenly the sense of what people are leaves one. I return him to the pool where he will acquire lustre.

Neville next—lying on his back staring up at the summer sky. He floated among us like a piece of thistledown, indolently haunting the sunny corner of the playing-field, not listening, yet not remote. It was through him that I have nosed round without ever precisely touching the Latin classics and have also derived some of those persistent habits of thought which make us irredeemably lop-sided—for instance about crucifixes, that they are the mark of the devil. Our half-loves and half hates and ambiguities on these points were to him indefensible treacheries. The swaying and sonorous Doctor, whom I made to sit swinging his braces over a gas-fire, was to him nothing but an instrument of the inquisition. So he turned with a passion that made up for his indolence upon Catullus, Horace, Lucretius, lying lazily dormant, yes, but regardant, noticing, with rapture, cricketers, while with a mind like the tongue of an anteater, rapid, dexterous, glutinous, he searched out every curl and twist of those Roman sentences, and sought out one person, always one person to sit beside.

The long skirts of the masters' wives would come swishing by, mountainous, menacing; and our hands would fly to our caps. Also, immense dullness would descend unbroken, monotonous. Nothing, nothing, nothing broke with its fin that leaden waste of waters. Nothing would happen to lift that weight of intolerable boredom. The terms went on. We grew; we changed; for, of course, we are animals. We are not always aware by any means; we breathe, eat, sleep automatically. We exist not only separately but in undifferentiated blobs of matter. With one scoop a whole brakeful of boys is swept up and goes cricketing, footballing. An army marches across Europe. We assemble in parks and halls and sedulously oppose any renegade (Neville, Louis, Rhoda) who sets up a separate existence. And I am so made that, while I hear one or two distinct melodies, such as Louis sings, or Neville, I am also drawn irresistibly to the sound of the chorus chanting its old, chanting its almost wordless, almost senseless song that comes across courts at night; which we hear now booming round us as cars and omnibuses take people to theatres. (Listen; the cars rush past this restaurant; now and then, down the river, a siren hoots, as a steamer makes for the sea.) If a bag man offers me snuff in a train I accept. I like the copious, shapeless, warm, not so very clever, but extremely easy and rather coarse aspect of things; the talk of men in clubs and public-houses, of miners half naked in 150 drawers—the forthright, perfectly unassuming, and without end in view except dinner, love, money and getting along tolerably; that which is without great hopes, ideals or anything of that kind; what is unassuming except to make a tolerably good job of it. I like all that. So I joined them, when Neville sulked or Louis, as I quite agree sublimely, turned on his heel.

Thus, not equally by any means or with order, but in great streaks my waxen waistcoat melted, here one drop, there another. Now through this transparency became visible those wondrous pastures, at first so moon-white, radiant, where no foot has been; meadows of the rose, the crocus, of the rock and the snake too; of the spotted and swart; the embarrassing, the binding and tripping up. One leaps out of bed, throws up the window; with what a whirr the birds rise! You know that sudden rush of wings, that exclamation, carol, and confusion; the riot and babble of voices; and all the drops are sparkling, trembling, as if the garden were a splintered mosaic, vanishing twinkling; not yet formed into one whole; and a bird sings close to the window. I heard those songs. I followed those phantoms. I saw Joans, Dorothys, Miriams, I forget their names, passing down avenues, stopping on the crest of bridges to look down into the river. And from among them rise one or two distinct figures, birds who sang with the rapt egotism of youth by the window; broke their snails on stones, dipped their beaks in sticky, viscous matter; hard, avid, remorseless; Jinny, Susan, Rhoda. They had been educated on the east coast or on the south coast. They had grown long pigtails and acquired the look of startled foals, which is the mark of adolescence.

Jinny was the first to come sidling up to the gate to eat sugar. She nipped it off the palms of one's hands very cleverly, but her ears were laid back as if she might bite. Rhoda was wild—Rhoda one never could catch. She was both frightened and clumsy. It was Susan who first became wholly woman, purely feminine. It was she who dropped on my face those scalding tears which are terrible, beautiful; both, neither. She was born to be the adored of poets, since poets require safety; someone who sits sewing, who says, "I hate, I love," who is neither comfortable nor prosperous, but has some quality in accordance with the high but unemphatic beauty of pure style which those who create poetry so particularly admire. Her father trailed from room to room and down flagged corridors in his flapping dressing-gown and worn slippers. On still nights a wall of water fell with a roar a mile off. The ancient dog could scarcely heave himself up on to his chair. And some witless servant could be heard laughing at the top of the house as she whirred the wheel of the sewing-machine round and round.

……

5.6 A Room of One's Own (1929)

A Room of One's Own, published in 1929, is considered to be her main contribution to feminist theory in early twentieth centuries. To some extent, it's the shaping of the characters that helped Woolf working out the spirits of what she really thought about feminism.

The dramatic setting of *A Room of One's Own* is that Woolf has been invited to lecture on the topic of Women and Fiction. She advances the thesis that "a woman must have money and a room of her own if she is to write fiction." Her essay is constructed as a partly-fictionalized narrative of the thinking that led her to adopt this thesis. She dramatizes that mental process in the character of an imaginary narrator ("call me Mary Beton, Mary Seton, Mary Carmichael or by any name you please—it is not a matter of any importance") who is in her same position, wrestling with the same topic.

The narrator begins her investigation at Oxbridge College, where she reflects on the different educational experiences available to men and women as well as on more material differences in their lives. She then spends a day in the British Library perusing the scholarship on women, all of which has written by men and all of which has been written in anger.

Throughout *A Room of One's Own*, the narrator emphasizes the fact that women are treated unequally in her society and that this is why they have produced less impressive works of writing than men. To illustrate her point, the narrator creates a woman named Judith Shakespeare, the imaginary twin sister of William Shakespeare. The narrator uses Judith to show how society systematically discriminates against women. Judith is just as talented as her brother William, but while his talents are recognized and encouraged by their family and the rest of their society, Judith's are underestimated and explicitly deemphasized. Judith writes, but she is secretive and ashamed of it. She is engaged at a fairly young age; when she begs not to have to marry, her beloved father beats her. She eventually commits suicide. The narrator invents the tragic figure of Judith to prove that a woman as talented as Shakespeare could never have achieved such success. Talent is an essential component of Shakespeare's success, but because women are treated so differently, a female Shakespeare would have fared quite differently even if she'd had as much talent as Shakespeare did.

The central point of *A Room of One's Own* is that every woman needs a room of her own—something men are able to enjoy without question. A room of her own would provide a woman with the time and the space to engage in uninterrupted writing time. During Woolf's time, women rarely enjoyed these luxuries. They remained

elusive to women, and, as a result, their art suffered. But Woolf is concerned with more than just the room itself. She uses the room as a symbol for many larger issues, such as privacy, leisure time, and financial independence, each of which is an essential component of the countless inequalities between men and women. Woolf predicts that until these inequalities are rectified, women will remain second-class citizens and their literary achievements will also be branded as such.

A Room of One's Own

The story:

Three

It was disappointing not to have brought back in the evening some important statement, some authentic fact. Women are poorer than men because—this or that. Perhaps now it would be better to give up seeking for the truth, and receiving on one's head an avalanche of opinion hot as lava, discoloured as dish-water. It would be better to draw the curtains; to shut out distractions; to light the lamp; to narrow the enquiry and to ask the historian, who records not opinions but facts, to describe under what conditions women lived, not throughout the ages, but in England, say, in the time of Elizabeth. For it is a perennial puzzle why no woman wrote a word of that extraordinary literature when every other man, it seemed, was capable of song or sonnet. What were the conditions in which women lived? I asked myself; for fiction, imaginative work that is, is not dropped like a pebble upon the ground, as science may be; fiction is like a spider's web, attached ever so lightly perhaps, but still attached to life at all four corners.

Often the attachment is scarcely perceptible; Shakespeare's plays, for instance, seem to hang there complete by themselves. But when the web is pulled askew, hooked up at the edge, torn in the middle, one remembers that these webs are not spun in mid-air by incorporeal creatures, but are the work of suffering human beings, and are attached to grossly material things, like health and money and the houses we live in.

I went, therefore, to the shelf where the histories stand and took down one of the latest, Professor Trevelyan's *The History of England*. Once more I looked up Women, found position of and turned to the pages indicated. 'Wife-beating', I read, 'was a recognized right of man, and was practised without shame by high as well as low... Similarly,' the historian goes on, 'the daughter who refused to marry the gentleman of her parents' choice was liable to be locked up, beaten and flung about the room, without any shock being inflicted on public opinion. Marriage was not an affair of personal affection, but of family avarice, particularly in the "chivalrous" upper classes....

Betrothal often took place while one or both of the parties was in the cradle, and marriage when they were scarcely out of the nurses charge. That was about 1470, soon after Chaucer's time. The next reference to the position of women is some two hundred years later, in the time of the Stuarts. It was still the exception for women of the upper and middle class to choose their own husbands, and when the husband had been assigned, he was lord and master, so far at least as law and custom could make him. Yet even so, Professor Trevelyan concludes, neither Shakespeare's women nor those of authentic seventeenth - century memoirs, like the Verneys and the Hutchinsons, seem wanting in personality and character.' Certainly, if we consider it, Cleopatra must have had a way with her; Lady Macbeth, one would suppose, had a will of her own; Rosalind, one might conclude, was an attractive girl. Professor Trevelyan is speaking no more than the truth when he remarks that Shakespeare's women do not seem wanting in personality and character. Not being a historian, one might go even further and say that women have burnt like beacons in all the works of all the poets from the beginning of time—Clytemnes-tra, Antigone, Cleopatra, Lady Macbeth, Phedre, Cressida, Ros-alind, Desdemona, the Duchess of Malfi, among the dramatists; then among the prose writers: Millamant, Clarissa, Becky Sharp, Anna Karenina, Emma Bovary, Madame de Guermantes—the names flock to mind, nor do they recall women 'lacking in personality and character.' Indeed, if woman had no existence save in the fiction written by men, one would imagine her a person of the utmost importance; very various; heroic and mean; splendid and sordid; infinitely beautiful and hideous in the extreme; as great as a man, some think even greater. But this is woman in fiction. In fact, as Professor Trevelyan points out, she was locked up, beaten and flung about the room.

A very queer, composite being thus emerges. Imaginatively she is of the highest importance; practically she is completely insignificant. She pervades poetry from cover to cover; she is all but absent from history. She dominates the lives of kings and conquerors in fiction; in fact she was the slave of any boy whose parents forced a ring upon her finger. Some of the most inspired words, some of the most profound thoughts in literature fall from her lips; in real life she could hardly read, could scarcely spell, and was the property of her husband. It was certainly an odd monster that one made up by reading the historians first and the poets afterwards—a worm winged like an eagle; the spirit of life and beauty in a kitchen chopping up suet. But these monsters, however amusing to the imagination, have no existence in fact. What one must do to bring her to life was to think poetically and prosaically at one and the same moment, thus keeping in touch with fact—that she is Mrs Martin, aged thirty-six, dressed in blue, wearing a black hat and brown shoes; but not losing sight of fiction either—that she is a vessel in which all sorts of spirits and forces are coursing and flashing perpetually. The moment, however, that one tries this method with the Elizabethan woman, one branch of illumination fails; one is held up by the scarcity of facts. One knows nothing detailed, nothing perfectly true and substantial about her. History scarcely mentions her. And I turned to Professor Trevelyan again to see what history meant to him.

Occasionally an individual woman is mentioned, an Elizabeth, or a Mary; a queen or a great lady. But by no-possible means could middle-class women with nothing but brains and character at their command have taken part in any one of the great movements which, brought together, constitute the historian's view of the past. Nor shall we find her in collection of anecdotes. Aubrey hardly mentions her. She never writes her own life and scarcely keeps a diary; there are only a handful of her letters in existence. She left no plays or poems by which we can judge her. What one wants, I thought—and why does not some brilliant student at Newnham or Girton supply it? —is a mass of information; at what age did she marry; how many children had she as a rule; what was her house like, had she a room to herself; did she do the cooking; would she be likely to have a servant? All these facts lie somewhere, presumably, in parish registers and account books; the life of the average Elizabethan woman must be scattered about somewhere, could one collect it and make a book. It would be ambitious beyond my daring, I thought, looking about the shelves for books that were not there, to suggest to the students of those famous colleges that they should rewrite history, though I own that it often seems a little queer as it is, unreal, lop-sided; but why should they not add a supplement to history, calling it, of course, by some inconspicuous name so that women might figure there without impropriety? For one often catches a glimpse of them in the lives of the great, whisking away into the back ground, concealing, I sometimes think, a wink, a laugh, perhaps a tear. After all, we have lives enough of Jane Austen; it scarcely seems necessary to consider again the influence of the tragedies of Joanna Baillie upon the poetry of Edgar Allan Poe; as for myself, I should not mind if the homes and haunts of Mary Russell Mitford were closed to the public for a century at least. But what I find deplorable, I continued, looking about the bookshelves again, is that nothing is known about women before the eighteenth century. I have no model in my mind to turn about this way and that. Here am I asking why women did not write poetry in the Elizabethan age, and I am not sure how they were educated; whether they were taught to write; whether they had sitting-rooms to themselves; how many women had children before they were twenty-one; what, in short, they did from eight in the morning till eight at night. They had no money evidently; according to Professor Trevelyan they were married whether they liked it or not before they were out of the nursery, at fifteen or sixteen very likely. It would have been extremely odd, even upon this showing, had one of them suddenly written the plays of Shakespeare, I concluded, and I thought of that old gentleman, who is dead now, but was a bishop, I think, who declared that it was impossible for any woman, past, present, or to come, to have the genius of Shakespeare. He wrote to the papers about it. He also told a lady who applied to him for information that cats do not as a matter of fact go to heaven, though they have, he added, souls of a sort. How much thinking those old gentlemen used to save one! How the borders of ignorance shrank back at their approach! Cats do not go to heaven. Women can not write the plays of Shakespeare.

5.7 The Mark on the Wall (1919)

The short piece *The Mark on the Wall*, published in 1919, was her first experimental novel considered to be her first successful achievements, because in which we see the extreme richness of the author's free imagination. In *The Mark on the Wall*, Woolf talks about the heroine's reveries when she notices a mark on the wall of her sitting room. About what the mark really is, her trains of thought jump from one thing to another. First of all, she thinks that the mark must have been made by a nail for a miniature of a lady, and imagines the lady's taste and the reason of her moving why her moving away. But then she suddenly doubts her speculation and thinks "if I got up and looked at it, ten to one I shouldn' t be able to say for certain; because once a thing' s done, one ever knows how it happened." At the moment, the heroine thinks of life and the world, and cannot help signing with feeling that life is full of accidents and dis orders : "Oh, dear me, the mystery of life; the inaccuracy of thought ! The ignorance of humanity !" Then, the heroine returns to the mark on the wall again, thinking, "it may be caused by some round black substance, such as a small rose leaf leftover from the summer". Following that, a series of associations occur to her—Shakespeare, the reign of Charles the First, Sunday afternoon walk, etc. And "In certain lights that mark on the wall seems actually to project from the wall", which subsequently makes her think of tombs. However, not very long the heroine comes to be deeply sunk into another series of free imagination, and what is more, she even thinks of an antiquary, are tired colonel and foot of a Chinese murderess at the local museum, etc.

Constantly stimulated by the particular external stimulus, the heroine opens up the world of speculation and wild imagination. Sometimes, she even does so by daring to deny the importance of long established convention, such as, which archbishop is followed by which archbishop, therefore, "let Nature comfort you".

But, after all, the heroine feels she must learn what on earth the mark on the wall is, and then she begins to associate it with something definite and real, such as " a plank in the sea", which makes her have " a satisfying sense of reality".

Obviously, It is a masterpiece of "free association", which is a striking feature of novel of the stream of consciousness. The heroine's mediation and thoughts constantly move far away from the particle of so called solid reality—what *the mark on the wall* really is.

So *the Mark on the Wall*, the earliest experimental short story of the stream of consciousness of Woolf, fully shows the typical features of the new technique of fiction writing and truthfully demonstrates the inner world of the character by describing her conscious, meditation, awareness and impression of the external world. Meanwhile, it is the truthful internal world of the character that reflects the reality and society. *The Mark on the Wall* becomes the media connecting the internal world and external one. The snail has hard outside shell and soft interior, which may be respectively, symbolized to the solid reality the consciousness. Therefore, it is likely that the snail is a perfect symbol of the combination of the two. In it, the author retreats out of the fiction, and makes the readers directly face the character and even the inner conscious of the character of the works. The short story only focuses on some fragments of thoughts flashes through the brain and instant impression occurs in the mind, but it portrays and captures "the moment of importance". Whether in style or in artistic from, *The Mark on the Wall* is the breakthrough to the traditional writing of fiction. It lays a solid foundation for her later novel of the stream of consciousness.

The Mark On the Wall

The story:

Perhaps it was the middle of January in the present that I first looked up and saw the mark on the wall. In order to fix a date it is necessary to remember what one saw. So now I think of the fire; the steady film of yellow light upon the page of my book; the three chrysanthemums in the round glass bowl on the mantelpiece. Yes, it must have been the winter time, and we had just finished our tea, for I remember that I was smoking a cigarette when I looked up and saw the mark on the wall for the first time. I looked up through the smoke of my cigarette and my eye lodged for a moment upon the burning coals, and that old fancy of the crimson flag flapping from the castle tower came into my mind, and I thought of the cavalcade of red knights riding up the side of the black rock. Rather to my relief the sight of the mark interrupted the fancy, for it is an old fancy, an automatic fancy, made as a child perhaps. The mark was a small round mark, black upon the white wall, about six or seven inches above the mantelpiece.

How readily our thoughts swarm upon a new object, lifting it a little way, as ants carry a blade of straw so feverishly, and then leave it ... If that mark was made by a nail, it can't have been for a picture, it must have been for a miniature the miniature of a lady with white powdered curls, powder-dusted cheeks, and lips like red carnations. A fraud of course, for the people who had this house before us would have chosen pictures in that way—an old picture for an old room. That is the sort of people they were very interesting people, and I think of them so often, in such queer places, because one will never see them again, never know what happened next. They wanted to leave this house because they wanted to change their style of furniture, so he said, and he was in process of saying that in his opinion art should have ideas behind it when we were torn asunder, as one is torn from the old lady about to pour out tea and the young man about to hit the tennis ball in the back

garden of the suburban villa as one rushes past in the train.

But as for that mark, I'm not sure about it; I don't believe it was made by a nail after all; it's too big, too round, for that. I might get up, but if I got up and looked at it, ten to one I shouldn't be able to say for certain; because once a thing's done, no one ever knows how it happened. Oh! dear me, the mystery of life; The inaccuracy of thought! The ignorance of humanity! To show how very little control of our possessions we have—what an accidental affair this living is after all our civilization—let me just count over a few of the things lost in one lifetime, beginning, for that seems always the most mysterious of losses—what cat would gnaw, what rat would nibble—three pale blue canisters of book-binding tools? Then there were the bird cages, the iron hoops, the steel skates, the Queen Anne coal-scuttle, the bagatelle board, the hand organ—all gone, and jewels, too. Opals and emeralds, they lie about the roots of turnips. What a scraping paring affair it is to be sure! The wonder is that I've any clothes on my back, that I sit surrounded by solid furniture at this moment. Why, if one wants to compare life to anything, one must liken it to being blown through the Tube at fifty miles an hour—landing at the other end without a single hairpin in one's hair! Shot out at the feet of God entirely naked! Tumbling head over heels in the asphodel meadows like brown paper parcels pitched down a shoot in the post office! With one's hair flying back like the tail of a race-horse. Yes, that seems to express the rapidity of life, the perpetual waste and repair; all so casual, all so haphazard . . .

But after life. The slow pulling down of thick green stalks so that the cup of the flower, as it turns over, deluges one with purple and red light. Why, after all, should one not be born there as one is born here, helpless, speechless, unable to focus one's eyesight, groping at the roots of the grass, at the toes of the Giants? As for saying which are trees, and which are men and women, or whether there are such things, that one won't be in a condition to do for fifty years or so. There will be nothing but spaces of light and dark, intersected by thick stalks, and rather higher up perhaps, rose-shaped blots of an indistinct colour—dim pinks and blues—which will, as time goes on, become more definite, become—I don't know what . . .

And yet that mark on the wall is not a hole at all. It may even be caused by some round black substance, such as a small rose leaf, left over from the summer, and I, not being a very vigilant housekeeper—look at the dust on the mantelpiece, for example, the dust which, so they say, buried Troy three times over, only fragments of pots utterly refusing annihilation, as one can believe. The tree outside the window taps very gently on the pane... I want to think quietly, calmly, spaciously, never to be interrupted, never to have to rise from my chair, to slip easily from one thing to another, without any sense of hostility, or obstacle. I want to sink deeper and deeper, away from the surface, with its hard separate facts. To steady myself, let me catch hold of the first idea that passes...Shakespeare... Well, he will do as well as another. A man who sat himself solidly in an arm-chair, and looked into the fire, so—A shower of ideas fell perpetually from some very high Heaven down through his mind. He leant his forehead on his hand, and people, looking in through the open door, —for this scene is supposed to take place on a summer's evening—But how dull this is, this historical fiction! It doesn't interest me at all. I wish I could hit upon a pleasant track of thought, a track indirectly reflecting credit upon myself, for those are the pleasantest thoughts, and very frequent even in the minds of modest mouse-coloured people, who believe genuinely that they dislike to hear their own praises. They are not thoughts directly praising oneself; that is the beauty of them; they are thoughts like this:

"And then I came into the room. They were discussing botany. I said how I'd seen a flower growing on a dust heap on the site of an old house in Kingsway. The seed, I said, must have been sown in the reign of Charles the First. What flowers grew in the reign of Charles the First?" I asked. Tall flowers with purple tassels to them perhaps and so it goes on. All the time I'm dressing up the figure of myself in my own mind, lovingly, stealthily, not openly adoring it, for if I did that, I should catch myself out, and stretch my hand at once for a book in self-protection. Indeed, it is curious how instinctively one protects the image of oneself from idolatry or any other handling that could make it ridiculous, or too unlike the original to be believed in any longer. Or is it not so very curious after all? It is a matter of great importance. Suppose the looking glass smashes, the image disappears, and the romantic figure with the green of forest depths all about it is there no longer, but only that shell of a person which is seen by other people—what an airless, shallow, bald, prominent world it becomes! A world not to be lived in. As we face each other in omnibuses and underground railways we are looking into the mirror that accounts for the vagueness, the gleam of glassiness, in our eyes. And the novelists in future will realize more and more the importance of these reflections, for of course there is not one reflection but an almost infinite number; those are the depths they will explore, those the phantoms they will pursue, leaving the description of reality more and more out of their stories, taking a knowledge of it for granted, as the Greeks did and Shakespeare perhaps—but these generalizations are very worthless. The military sound of the word is enough. It recalls leading articles, cabinet ministers—a whole class of things indeed which as a child one thought the thing itself, the standard thing, the real thing, from which one could not depart save at the risk of nameless damnation. Generalizations bring back somehow Sunday in London, Sunday afternoon walks, Sunday luncheons, and also ways of speaking of the dead, clothes, and habits—like the habit of sitting all together in one room until a certain hour, although nobody liked it. There was a rule for everything. The rule for tablecloths at that particular period was that they should be made of tapestry with little yellow compartments marked upon them, such as you may see in photographs of the carpets in the corridors of the royal palaces. Tablecloths of a different kind were not real tablecloths. How shocking, and yet how wonderful it was to discover that these real things, Sunday luncheons, Sunday walks, country houses, and tablecloths were not entirely real, were indeed half phantoms, and the damnation which visited the disbeliever in them was only a sense of illegitimate freedom. What now takes the place of those things I wonder, those real standard things? Men perhaps, should you be a woman; the masculine point of view which governs our lives, which sets the standard, which establishes Whitaker's Table of Precedency, which has become, I suppose, since the war half a phantom to many men and women, which soon—one may hope, will be laughed into the dustbin where the phantoms go, the mahogany sideboards and the Landseer prints, Gods and Devils, Hell and so forth, leaving us all with an intoxicating sense of illegitimate freedom—if freedom exists . . .

In certain lights that mark on the wall seems actually to project from the wall. Nor is it entirely circular. I cannot be sure, but it seems to cast a perceptible shadow, suggesting that if I ran my finger down that strip of the wall it would, at a certain point, mount and descend a small tumulus, a smooth tumulus like those barrows on the South Downs which are, they say, either tombs or camps. Of the two I should prefer them to be tombs, desiring melancholy like most Englishman, and finding it natural at the end of a walk to think of the bones stretched beneath the turf . . . There must be some book about it. Some antiquary must have dug up those bones and given them a name . . . What sort of a man is an antiquary, I wonder? Retired Colonels for the most part, I dare say, leading parties of aged labourers to the top here, examining clods of earth and stone, and getting into correspondence with the neighbouring clergy, which, being opened at breakfast time, gives them a feeling of importance, and the comparison of arrow-heads necessitates cross-country journeys to the county towns, an agreeable necessity both to them and to their elderly wives, who wish to make plum jam or to clean out the study, and have every reason for keeping that great question of the camp or the tomb in perpetual suspension, while the Colonel himself feels agreeably philosophic in accumulating evidence on both sides of the question. It is true that he does finally incline to believe in the camp; and, being opposed, indites a pamphlet which he is about to read at the quarterly meeting of the local society when a stroke lays him low, and his last conscious thoughts are not of wife or child, but of the camp and that arrowhead there, which is now in the case at the local museum, together with the foot of a Chinese murderess, a handful of Elizabethan nails, a great many Tudor clay pipes, a piece of Roman pottery, and the wine-glass that Nelson drank out of—proving I really don't know what.

Nothing is proved and nothing is known. If I were to get up at this very moment and ascertain that the mark on the wall is really—what shall we say? —the head of a gigantic old nail, driven in two hundred years ago, which has now, owing to the patient attrition of many generations of housemaids, revealed its head above the coat of paint, and is taking its first view of modern life in the sight of a white-walled fire-lit room, what should I gain? —Knowledge? Matter for further speculation? I can think sitting still as well as standing up. And what is knowledge? What are our learned men save the descendants of witches and hermits who crouched in caves and in woods brewing herbs, interrogating shrew-mice and writing down the language of the stars? The less we honour them as our superstitions dwindle and our respect for beauty and health of mind increases ... Yes, one could imagine a very pleasant world. A quiet, spacious world, with the flowers so red and blue in the open fields. A world without professors or specialists or house-keepers with the profiles of policemen, a world which one could slice with one's thought as a fish slices the water with his fin, grazing the stems of the water-lilies, hanging suspended over nests of white sea eggs ... How peaceful it is drown here, rooted in the centre of the world and gazing up through the grey waters, with their sudden gleams of light, and their reflections—if it were not for Whitaker's Almanack—if it were not for the *Table of Precedency*!

I must jump up and see for myself what that mark on the wall really is—a nail, a rose-leaf, a crack in the wood?

Here is nature once more at her old game of self-preservation. This train of thought, she perceives, is threatening mere waste of energy, even some collision with reality, for who will ever be able to lift a finger against Whitaker's Table of Precedency? The Archbishop of Canterbury is followed by the Lord High Chancellor; the Lord High Chancellor is followed by the Archbishop of York. Everybody follows somebody, such is the philosophy of Whitaker; and the great thing is to know who follows whom. Whitaker knows, and let that, so Nature counsels, comfort you, instead of enraging you; and if you can't be comforted, if you must shatter this hour of peace, think of the mark on the wall.

I understand Nature's game—her prompting to take action as a way of ending any thought that threatens to excite or to pain. Hence, I suppose, comes our slight contempt for men of action—men, we assume, who don't think. Still, there's no harm in putting a full stop to one's disagreeable thoughts by looking at a mark on the wall.

Indeed, now that I have fixed my eyes upon it, I feel that I have grasped a plank in the sea; I feel a satisfying sense of reality which at once turns the two Archbishops and the Lord High Chancellor to the shadows of shades. Here is something definite, something real. Thus, waking from a midnight dream of horror, one hastily turns on the light and lies quiescent, worshiping the chest of drawers, worshiping solidity, worshiping reality, worshiping the impersonal world which is a proof of some existence other than ours. That is what one wants to be sure of ... Wood is a pleasant thing to think about. It comes from a tree; and trees grow, and we don't know how they grow. For years and years they grow, without paying any attention to us, in meadows, in forests, and by the side of rivers—all things one likes to think about. The cows swish their tails beneath them on hot afternoons; they paint rivers so green that when a moorhen dives one expects to see its feathers all green when it comes up again. I like to think of the fish balanced against the stream like flags blown out; and of water-beetles slowly raiding domes of mud upon the bed of the river. I like to think of the tree itself: —first the close dry sensation of being wood; then the grinding of the storm; then the slow, delicious ooze of sap. I like to think of it, too, on winter's nights standing in the empty field with all leaves close-furled, nothing tender exposed to the iron bullets of the moon, a naked mast upon an earth that goes tumbling, tumbling, all night long. The song of birds must sound very loud and strange in June; and how cold the feet of insects must feel upon it, as they make laborious progresses up the creases of the bark, or sun themselves upon the thin green awning of the leaves, and look straight in front of them with diamond-cut red eyes ...

One by one the fibres snap beneath the immense cold pressure of the earth, then the last storm comes and, falling, the highest branches drive deep into the ground again. Even so, life isn't done with; there are a million patient, watchful lives still for a tree, all over the world, in bedrooms, in ships, on the pavement, lining rooms, where men and women sit after tea, smoking cigarettes. It is full of peaceful thoughts, happy thoughts, this tree. I should like to take each one separately—but something is getting in the way ... Where was I? What has it all been about? A tree? A river? The Downs? Whitaker's Almanack? The fields of asphodel? I can't remember a thing. Everything's moving, falling, slipping, vanishing ... There is a vast upheaval of matter. Someone is standing over me and saying—

"I'm going out to buy a newspaper."

"Yes?"

"Though it's no good buying newspapers ... Nothing ever happens. Curse this war; ... All the same, I don't see why we should have a snail on our wall."

"Ah, the mark on the wall! It was a snail."

References

[1] Abrams H. The York & London: Norton Anthology of English Literature [M]. New Norton & Company, 1993.

[2] Bell, Quentin. Virginia Woolf: A Biography [M]. Harcourt Brace Jovanovich, 1972.

[3] Deborah Cameron. Feminism and Linguistic Theory [M]. The Macmillan Press, 1985.

[4] DiBattista, Maria. Virginia Woolf's Major Novels: The Fables of Anon [M]. New Haven, Conn.: Yale University Press, 1980.

[5] Ferrer, Daniel. Virginia Woolf and the madness of language [M]. London; New York: Routledge, 1990.

[6] James, William. The Principles of Psychology [M]. Boston: The President and Fellows of Harvard College, 1983.

[7] Jill K. Conway, Susan C. Bourque, Joan W. Scott, Learning about Women Gender, Politics, and Power [M]. The University of Michigan Press, 1989.

[8] Joyce, James. Ulysses, Harmondsworth, Middlesex [M]. New Work: The Bodley Head, 1986.

[9] Lee, Hermione. The Novel of Virginia Woolf [M]. London: Methuen and Co, Ltd., 1977.

[10] Lodge, David. The Modes of Modern Writing: Metaphor, Metonymy, and the Typology of Modern Literature [M]. Ithaca: Cornell University Press, 1977.

[11] Moi, Toril. Sexual/Texual Politics: Feminist Literary Theory [M]. Methuen, 1985.

[12] Roe, Sue. Writing and Gender: Roe, Sue&Sellers, Susan. The Cambridge Companion To Virginia Woolf [M]. Shanghai: Shanghai Foreign Language Education Press, 2001.

[13] Sue Soe and Susan Sellers [M]. Shanghai: Shanghai Foreign Language Education

Press, 2001.

[14] Virginia Woolf. Mrs. Dalloway [M]. London: Hogarth Press, 1990.

[15] Virginia Woolf. Orlando. Hertfordshire: Wordsworth Editions Limited Cumberland House. 1995.

[16] Virginia Woolf's Writing Practice [M]. New York: Saint Martin's Press, Inc., 1990.

[17] Virginia Woolf . The Mark on the Wall refers to http: //www. bartleby. com/85/8. html.

[18] Virginia Woolf. The Mark On The Wall, refers to http: //www. feedbooks. com.

[19] Virginia Woolf. The Reader, New York and London: Harcourt Brace Jovanovich, p. 154.

[20] Virginia Woolf. The Waves, refers to http : //www. feedbooks. com.

[21] Virginia Woolf. To the Lighthouse. Foreword by Eudora Welty. San Diego: Harvestl Harcourt Brace Jovanovich, 1989 (1920): 19-20.

[22] Virginia Woolf. To the Lighthouse [M]. Oxford: Oxford U. P., 1992.

[23] Whitworth, Michael. Virginia Woolf and Modernism. [M]. Shanghai: Shanghai Foreign Language Education Press, 2001.

[24] 高奋，鲁彦．近20年国内弗吉尼亚·伍尔夫研究述评 [J]. 外国文学研究，2004 (5).

[25] 瞿世镜．伍尔夫研究 [M]. 上海：上海文艺出版社，1988.

[26] 瞿世镜．意识流小说理论 [M]. 成都：四川文艺出版社，1989.

[27] 李维屏．英美意识流小说 [M]. 上海：上海外语教育出版社，1996.

[28] 贝蒂·弗里丹．女性的奥秘 [M]. 程锡麟，朱徽，王晓路译，哈尔滨：北方文艺出版社，1999.

[29] 童小英．叙述学 [M]. 北京：社会科学文献出版社，2001.

[30] 伍厚恺．弗吉尼亚·伍尔夫：存在的瞬间 [M]. 成都：四川人民出版社，1999.

[31] 弗吉尼亚·伍尔夫．到灯塔去 [M]. 瞿世镜译，上海：上海文艺出版社，2000.

[32] 弗吉尼亚·伍尔夫．自己的一间屋 [M]. 贾辉丰译．北京：人民文学出版社，2000.

[33] 特里·伊格尔顿．当代西方文学理论［M］王逢振译．北京：中国社会科学出版社，1988.

[34] 张秉真，张安祺，杨慧林．西方文艺理论史［M］．北京：中国人民大学出版社，1999.

[35] 张京媛．当代女性主义文学批评［M］．北京：北京大学出版社，1995.

[36] 张岩冰．女权主义文论［M］．济南：山东教育出版社，2002.

[37] 赵毅衡．当说者被说的时候——比较叙述学导论［M］．北京：中国人民大学出版社，1998.